THE MIGHTY
747

Jim Eames has been involved with airlines since he began work as an aviation writer in the 1960s. He has been a ministerial press secretary and aviation adviser to governments and a senior executive with Qantas. He is the author of nine books including *Taking to the Skies: Daredevils, heroes and hijackers, Australian flying stories from the Catalina to the Jumbo, The Flying Kangaroo: Great untold stories of Qantas . . . the heroic, the hilarious and the sometimes plain strange* and *Courage in the Skies: The untold story of Qantas, its brave men and women and their extraordinary role in World War II.*

THE MIGHTY
747

AUSTRALIA'S QUEEN
OF THE SKIES

JIM EAMES

ALLEN&UNWIN
SYDNEY • MELBOURNE • AUCKLAND • LONDON

This edition published in 2022
First published in 2022

Every effort has been made to trace the holders of copyright material. If you have
any information concerning copyright material in this book please contact the
publishers at the address below.

Allen & Unwin
Cammeraygal Country
83 Alexander Street
Crows Nest NSW 2065
Australia
Phone: (61 2) 8425 0100
Email: info@allenandunwin.com
Web: www.allenandunwin.com

*Allen & Unwin acknowledges the Traditional Owners of the Country on which we
live and work. We pay our respects to all Aboriginal and Torres Strait Islander
Elders, past and present.*

A catalogue record for this
book is available from the
National Library of Australia

ISBN 978 1 76087 711 8

Set in 12.5/18 pt Adobe Caslon Pro by Midland Typesetters, Australia
Printed and bound in Australia by Pegasus Media & Logistics

10 9 8 7 6 5 4 3

CONTENTS

A sentimental favourite vii

1. The father of the 747 1
2. Temptations and doubts 10
3. 'It's Boeing' 20
4. The Jet Base 27
5. Ready to fly 32
6. A tale of two cities 39
7. The first QF Boeing 747 touches down 44
8. It's all about the engines 55
9. Stormy skies ahead—and not just with the weather 65
10. 'The pilots' airline' 69
11. Politics and ministers 79
12. A pilot's view 98
13. They came in all shapes 104
14. And they came in all sizes 109
15. Christenings—a tale of politics and media junkets 126
16. Hi ho, hi ho, it's into the air we go 136
17. Into the record books—non-stop across the world 141

18.	Keeping 'em flying	153
19.	Keeping watch in the cockpit	163
20.	'Luck's a fortune'	174
21.	The humour of it all	184
22.	Not just any passengers	199
23.	The Antarctic airline	212
24.	The return of the diggers	219
25.	The sound of gunfire in Mogadishu	224
26.	The 'Oshkosh Express'	229
27.	'This 747 is a whole new ball game'	233
28.	Rearranging the deckchairs	240
29.	Saving our 'Queen of the Skies'	247
30.	The final farewell	256
Reflections		262
Acknowledgements		267
Sources		271

A SENTIMENTAL FAVOURITE

At first sight, on the ground, it can present a slightly ungainly shape. Its upper-deck bubble seems somehow out of character with the sleek examples of high-speed air transport we have come to know since the birth of the jet age.

But first impressions can be misleading. Once in the air, its shape quickly transforms into an image that not only captures the gracefulness of flight but also has created indelible memories for millions of us. This is the aeroplane that opened up the world for generations of Australians, providing them with an opportunity to venture overseas for the first time. Among them were many thousands of war migrants who would finally reconnect with their families scattered all over the world.

But the Boeing 747 in Qantas service reached further than that, creating probably one of the largest gatherings of dedicated followers of any aircraft to have flown Australian skies.

Much of its reputation, of course, had to do with Australia's geographic remoteness. It was this remoteness that carved out Australia's space in the skies of the world, giving Australians such a deep affinity with aeroplanes and the early aviators who flew them. It also partly explains why certain of the 747's predecessors—such as the Douglas DC-3 and the Constellation—claimed a special place in the hearts of past generations.

Looking beyond its passengers and more deeply at the 747 itself, however, one finds an aeroplane that draws a very sentimental response from those who spent their lives working closely with it: the air crews and cabin crews who flew in it day and night, those who maintained and sold its seats, and even those in the air traffic control towers who cleared it for take-off and landing.

It's also a story of groundbreaking airport runway and terminal requirements, of negotiating the often-political international air services agreements and overflight rights between sovereign nations, and of meeting the challenges of advances in engine technology. Along with the 747 came a new era of in-flight entertainment and, for that matter, innovations in how the meals served to passengers made it onto their fold-down trays somewhere over the mid-Pacific.

But if the story of the 747 in Qantas demonstrates anything, it is that an airline is really about people rather than just the machinery that brings the excitement, speed and comfort—and, of course, occasionally the excitement and risk. So, while the last Qantas Boeing 747 departed Australian skies just a few weeks short of its 50th anniversary with the airline, it left a lasting legacy. That legacy had its origins many thousands of miles away on the far side of the world.

1
THE FATHER OF
THE 747

The aircraft that would go on to make history and become affectionately known as 'The Queen of the Skies' was actually born out of disappointment. Indeed, had Boeing not lost out to its competitor Lockheed in a bid to build a military transport aircraft for the US Air Force, the 747 might never have been built—at least not in the form we have come to know it.

As time passes, and as history often confirms, myths can be created out of the most basic of facts. One such myth is that Boeing simply converted the design it had developed for the US Air Force military transport into the 747. It is true that Lockheed won the air force contract, with the aircraft that would become known as the C-5A Galaxy, but the design Boeing had submitted for a high-wing aircraft bore little resemblance to the eventual 747 beyond its sheer size. By the time the C-5A decision was announced, however, a new design—the Boeing 747—was already on the drawing board.

Its real origins go back even further. Some would even suggest it has links to that other iconic aircraft, the 707, back in a time when Boeing was largely known not for its civilian aircraft but for the production of military aircraft. It had produced iconic versions of that genre, like the B-17 bombers that flew above most of the battlefronts of World War II. Boeing's military signature would continue post war with the development of aircraft such as the B-47 and the B-52, both playing roles in the Cold War and the Korean conflict.

But when it came to airliners, it was Lockheed, Boeing's major competitor, that paved the way to the development of aircraft specifically designed for civilian use, particularly the Super Constellation in the mid-fifties. Before then, it had been a matter of converting ex-military variants for civilian use, such as the Douglas DC-3 and DC-4, and Britain's Lancaster.

As with the eventual 747, the Boeing 707 was a gamble. It would be the first big US step into the commercial jet age, a risk that was destined to enter aviation folklore even before the first one had been sold.

***

It happened in Seattle one morning in 1954, as Boeing chief Bill Allen played host to a gathering of US airline chief executives aboard a yacht on Lake Washington. Allen was attempting to sell them what he believed was his company's four-engined jet masterpiece, designed to cut propeller-driven airliner schedules in half.

The aeroplane that Boeing's chief test pilot Tex Johnston

was flying towards the luxury yacht that morning hadn't even yet earned the numerals '707'. Bearing a relatively plain dusty-brown-and-yellow livery, it was simply known as the Dash 80 prototype model.

Peering proudly skywards, Allen saw the Dash 80 climb gently as it approached them, only to watch in sudden horror as the big jet dipped sideways into a barrel roll. Unbeknown to Allen, Johnston had decided to show those airline fellows below just how good he believed this aeroplane was. Not satisfied with doing it once, he then repeated the manoeuvre, cheekily waggling his aircraft's wings as he flew off.

Any comment Allen might have made to his colleagues on the yacht is not recorded but his dressing down of Johnston back at the Boeing factory the next morning is well known, underlined with the comment that the entire plan for the Boeing 707 could have ended right there. Tex Johnston wasn't fazed. He simply repeated that he knew what his aircraft could do, and it was his idea of salesmanship!

Such was the 707's success that versions of it—and its main opposition, the Douglas DC-8—would dominate the long-range domestic and international airline market for years to come. Until, of course, the mid-1960s, when the US Air Force went looking for a large transport aircraft and once again Boeing would take the ultimate gamble. This time, however, not only would they be risking the very existence of the company on one aeroplane, but they would have to confront a large dose of scepticism on the part of many of the airlines they hoped would purchase it.

***

Over the long years of its history, many would claim owner-ship of part of the original idea to build the 'jumbo', as it became known. But there is no denying the four men who played the biggest roles in bringing it into existence.

The two of the four with the most significant commercial reputations at stake were Bill Allen, who had shuddered at Tex Johnston's barrel roll over Lake Washington, and a man who could match Allen's deal-making ability across any table—his counterpart at Pan American Airways, Juan Trippe.

Trippe was himself a pioneer in commercial aviation, having taken a floatplane service between Florida and Havana, Cuba, in the late 1920s and turned Pan Am into a pioneer of the jet age, and a recognisable flagship of US foreign policy. Winning Trippe over for an order of 25 aircraft in a deal worth more than $500 million was a masterstroke by Allen because he knew that once Pan Am had signed on the dotted line, other airlines would follow.

The subsequent exchange between Allen and Malcolm Stamper, a long-time Boeing executive, as Allen handed Stam-per the overall responsibility for the 747 late in 1966, has since become Boeing folklore:

'How would you like to build an airplane—in fact, the biggest airplane in the world?'
'Mr Allen, the only airplane I've ever built had rubber bands on it.'

Fully aware that the company's future would be riding on it, Stamper accepted the challenge and became the third member of the team that brought the 747 into existence.

Everything about the Boeing 747 project was big—and some of the statistics associated with it are indeed mind-boggling. For a start, building an aeroplane 70 metres long and with a tail six storeys high to carry 400 people would require the construction of a plant almost 400,000 square metres in size, with a width of more than a kilometre and a half. Built in Everett, outside Seattle, it would be the largest factory in the world. As for the 747 itself, it represented 70,000 engineering drawings, 270 kilometres of wiring and over four million parts.

But it would be the fourth member of the key team, along with Allen, Trippe and Stamper, who would be most directly responsible for the new aircraft, and would eventually become known throughout the entire aviation industry as 'The Father of the 747'. This was Joe Sutter, the chief design and project engineer.

Sutter might have grown up in a suburb overlooking Boeing Field at Renton, Seattle, but he'd considered his first job at Boeing as only temporary. After serving in the US Navy in World War II, he only accepted a job at Boeing while he considered a full-time offer from the Douglas Aircraft Company in California. It was the start of a 40-year career with Boeing during which he would also be deeply involved in the production of the 707, the 727 and the 737.

The achievement of these four men—creating the world's largest civilian airliner from conception to roll-out in just twenty months, within a company already deeply involved in production of the Boeing 727-200, the 737 and a planned supersonic transport to match the British–French Concorde—earned Stamper, Sutter and those who worked with them the title 'The Incredibles'. In time, Joe Sutter became the most sought-after official at Boeing when world airline leaders came to Seattle to discuss the progress of their aircraft on Boeing's production line.

Charles Reynolds, in charge of Boeing's 747 airline customer relations at the time, later described Sutter as 'the heart and soul' of the 747 program: 'He would go anywhere the sales department needed him, to push the plane as part of an airline's fleet.' Reynolds would later be appointed Boeing's Sydney-based Australian representative, and he experienced firsthand Sutter's influence when it came to Qantas. Once, when he asked what the Qantas team needed for an upcoming visit to Seattle by the airline's general manager Keith Hamilton, he was told, 'Just make sure Sutter is at all the significant meetings and dinners.'

Reynolds confesses many similar requests came from other airlines but it was often Qantas that captured more of Boeing's attention. As he points out, this wasn't some Northern Hemisphere airline that could easily toddle an aircraft back to Seattle to sort out a problem: 'Australia was 10,000 miles away and they needed to be much more self-sufficient than the others.'

Not that high regard for Sutter was restricted to those who purchased his aircraft. One Qantas executive remembers the presence of Australian golfing great Greg Norman attracting considerable attention among other first-class passengers en route to the United States. There were a few wry smiles among them when the captain came down for his customary cabin walk-through, and walked past Norman to sit down for a chat with Sutter.

Many years later Sutter, too, would confess he had a special regard for Qantas as a Boeing 747 customer:

> I think Qantas took a very bold step for a small airline to decide to compete with the Pan Americans, the TWAs and the Lufthansas. It took a lot of courage for Qantas to launch the 747 in that part of the world. They not only knew what they wanted, though—they also knew what they needed and they were not shy about asking for it. Because we came to know what they needed and how to tackle any problems which arose, we paid a lot of attention to Qantas.

Neither was Sutter ever threatened by the inevitable cut and thrust at the executive level of a company like Boeing. 'He knew the Boeing pecking order as much as he knew the airlines,' Charles Reynolds confirms. Others at Boeing remember an engineer who, along with a willingness to share credit with his team, would quietly keep his own counsel at meetings, waiting to hear everyone else out until it came time to reach a decision, which would be announced in a firm, no-nonsense way.

Nor was Sutter prepared to bow to pressure when his pet project was threatened—and threatened it was, with a Boeing board nervously looking at the requirement to service millions of dollars of bank debt while it watched costs build to around US$5 million a day, with no prospect of a return until the company could begin to sell the end result.

On one occasion, when money began to tighten and a Bill Allen edict came down the line to cut costs, Sutter refused to accept a reduction in his engineering force, instead storming out of the meeting, later confessing he fully expected to be sacked. Not only did Sutter keep his job, but he kept his work-force as well.

***

As the months passed, and the first of the 747s took to the air, problems began to develop in the engines that powered the giant, threatening to place the whole future of the aeroplane in jeopardy. At one stage, Pan Am had five of their first aircraft out of service with faulty engines. Nor did it help when news photos began to appear of a flight line of brand-new yet undelivered Boeing 747s sitting sterile on Seattle's flight line—all with weight-balancing concrete slabs instead of engines hanging from their wings.

For Boeing and Pratt & Whitney, one of the 'big-three' aero-engine manufacturers, based in Connecticut, the dilemma became known as the 'ovalising' of the engines' skin casing, which created a distortion that caused the turbine blades to rub against the interior of the engine cowling. Eventually the problem would be overcome, but not before relationships between the two companies neared breaking point. Over time, due to its particular long-range route structure, Qantas's earliest 747s too would suffer engine problems, with similar cost implications.

Despite such early setbacks, Juan Trippe's Pan Am, as launch customer, would enjoy the worldwide prestige and accompanying media glamour of being the first to take the Boeing 747 to the four corners of the globe. Qantas former senior cabin crew member Ed Ronsisvalle remembers his first sight of a Pan Am 747 in Hong Kong. When Ed asked a ground-crew worker what he thought of it, he was told they had named it 'The Saviour'. He asked why, and the crew member elaborated: 'When most people see it for the first time, all they seem to say is "Jesus Christ!"'

When, on the afternoon of 4 October 1970, a crowd estimated at around 10,000 watched Pan Am's Boeing 747 touch down at Mascot for the first time, the 747 in Qantas colours was still almost twelve months away. But much had changed since those early days in the 1960s when the Australian airline had viewed the prospect of such a giant of the skies with a healthy degree of scepticism.

2
TEMPTATIONS
AND DOUBTS

Boeing's initial offer of the 747 to Qantas had come in 1966, when Cedric Turner was in the chief executive's chair and when the airline was looking at replacing its Boeing 707-138s with the larger -338 versions. For Qantas, however, it was not only too soon to consider a 707 replacement, but there was the further complication of the prospect of a super-sonic transport aircraft, either of the British–French Concorde or the US's own version, just around the corner.

So the initial Boeing offer was allowed to lapse while Qantas continued to ponder how it would handle the different requirements of these two technological developments and, most importantly, the threat of overcapacity they might present. Fortunately for Qantas, this early hesitation would play to its advantage, allowing the company to watch as Pratt & Whitney and Boeing struggled to overcome the engine problems and the 747's initial operating-range capability.

Australia's geographical location and the long stage lengths of Qantas's route structure meant that, in those early days, many in the airline, including Turner's successor as chief executive Bert Ritchie, harboured doubts about the engines. They pressed both Pratt & Whitney and Boeing for more thrust from the engines and greater range, lessons Qantas had learned in the early days of its 707 services across the Pacific.

Those at Boeing, like Sutter, realised that this was a case of history repeating itself, as far as Qantas and Boeing were concerned. Back in the early 707 days of the mid-1950s, Qantas had been only the fifth airline (after American, Air France, Sabena and Lufthansa) to order the 707.

Back then, in Qantas's case, the 707 had been all about 'range', or the ability to tackle those long sectors that were a critical part of its network. What Boeing was offering Qantas was a 707 primarily suited to the domestic and intercontinental demands of the big American airlines, which were more interested in Boeing stretching the aircraft to better suit their passenger loads.

Qantas, on the other hand, faced an over-water distance of more than 5000 kilometres between Fiji's Nadi airport and Honolulu. Any projected redesign of the 707 would mean the larger aircraft would still be unable to operate over such a distance due to the limitations presented by Nadi's relatively short 2100-metre runway—a phenomenon that would become known in airline parlance as the 'Nadi bump'. What Qantas required, in contrast to Boeing's larger airline customers, was in fact a shorter version of the aircraft with additional engine power to get it airborne out of Nadi.

And that's exactly what Boeing came up with. First, it agreed to take 3 metres out of the length of the fuselage, then it upgraded its Pratt & Whitney engines to match the more powerful military versions. Thus, with such a technological confluence, Qantas in 1959 became the first non-US airline outside the US to put the 707 into service.

Now, ten years on, when facing the introduction of the 747, Qantas once again had to be sure Boeing produced an aeroplane that was beyond the operating distance requirements of their Northern Hemisphere customers. At every opportunity, Qantas pointed out even the airline's closest destination in Asia, Indonesia's Bali, was as far away from Sydney as London was from New York.

Even before the first flight of the 747 prototype in 1969, some in Qantas took convincing on the economics. An early Boeing offer on the later B version was rejected, despite Boeing's argument that the additional cost of the B version would bring with it economic and performance advantages over Pan Am's A model.

Added to this was the maintenance problem. Qantas co-founder Hudson Fysh had overcome a similar problem in the immediate pre-war days, when he insisted on establishing his own maintenance support base for the Empire flying boats in Australia. Now, as with the United Kingdom almost 50 years before, Qantas knew it was too far away from Boeing and Pratt & Whitney to be anything other than self-sufficient when it came to engineering and maintenance support.

***

Among the doubters was Qantas technical director Bob Walker. Walker saw the problems close up and he saw them early, back when Boeing was using the original 747 drawing-board concept during their competition with Lockheed for the US Air Force contract. Walker was particularly concerned when it came to engines:

> In the very early days [Boeing would] come down every two or three months and tell us what they were doing, and we'd keep saying, 'No matter what you do we will need four engines,' as we didn't want to have to worry about reliability with only one engine working. With that we couldn't even fly a two-engine aircraft across the Tasman.
>
> Their military said they'd want four engines anyway so eventually they came to us with one called the 747. But the thing was as big as a Manly ferry. So when they told us they were thinking of around 350 passengers and something the size of a Manly ferry, we said, 'Go away!' This was the very early days, of course, and we only wanted something for about 100 passengers.

Walker, renowned throughout the industry for his sense of humour, has a light-hearted recall of the initial exchange with Boeing. 'Look,' he told them, 'maybe if Air New Zealand, or maybe Singapore Airlines, or us got together, we'd buy one of them!'

While Walker might have been half-joking, it bears remembering that these were the days before cheap excursion fares, which would bring an unprecedented surge in air travel, particularly between Australia and Asia and Europe.

Eventually, however, even for Walker, the sums began to add up. 'With the 707 then moving from 90 passengers to 120, we thought we could make the 747 pay with a passenger load factor initially of about 30 per cent, so we decided to buy four.'

Walker recalls his awe on his first trip to Seattle to look at the 747 mock-ups. 'This thing had double aisles and my first thought was it might not get off the ground, but gradually you became used to it and its four undercarriage legs. Even when you finally saw it flying it looked very slow because it was so big. They told us if they sold 200 they could break even.'

Now, of course, it was up to Qantas to convince the Australian government to produce the funds. Then came one of those quirky misunderstandings that can occur in the most delicate of financial deals. Having placed the Qantas financial requirements before Treasury and the World Bank, the airline's chairman Sir Roland Wilson was shocked when the signal came back from the World Bank that they were 'not ready to finalise the finance'.

The story goes that Wilson, ever the public servant, was reluctant to get on the phone to the Bank and query the note. Some weeks passed before, to his surprise, the Bank asked why he hadn't taken up the loan offer.

It turned out there'd been a typo—with 'not' substituted for 'now'.

Inevitably, Bob Walker would have his own spin on the issue, suggesting the 'typo' worked in Qantas's favour: 'The delay probably helped in the long run as Pan Am continued to get the bugs out of it!'

Just what those 'bugs' were might have been helpful for Qantas to know, but the airline was having trouble finding out much about them, forcing Australia's Department of Civil Aviation chief Sir Donald Anderson to ask his own representative in Washington, Australia's civil air attaché Rex Banks, for help. A former journalist, Banks didn't take long to find out that Pan Am had compiled a report on the first six months of its 747 operations. When he set out to find it, however, he soon learned that Pan Am wanted to keep the report a closely guarded secret.

Spurred on by his old journalistic instincts, Banks widened the search via a close colleague in the US Congress who he knew had excellent contacts in the industry. 'Thanks to him I had the report, which covered all aspects of the 747 operations, both economic and mechanical, on my desk within a few hours!' Banks recalls.

Looking back, Banks suggests the incident demonstrated the good relations Australia had with the US civil aviation industry at the time. This was in striking contrast to the confrontation just over the horizon, which would see the two nations clash angrily over Qantas's plans to use its 747 as part of its traffic rights between Australia and the US.

***

While the concept of the 747 might have been occupying Qantas's mind as the sixties progressed, still lingering in the background was the continuing development of the concept of the supersonic transport, or SST. Unlike the 747, this was not primarily about the number of passengers but about speed.

As far back as 1962, Cedric Turner had briefed the Qantas board on an SST designed to cruise at Mach 2—twice the speed of sound. Once again, as had occurred in the transition from the propeller-driven Constellation to the 707 jet, this development was capable of slashing flight times between continents. While the British, through BOAC, were encouraging Qantas to become involved in discussions on the Anglo-French Concorde, the US was looking at an even larger and faster aircraft entering service around mid-1970. Some estimates put the total SST world market at around 350 aircraft.

But ominous signs around noise factors were already being recognised, in particular the impact of the sonic boom created by shock waves over the ground surface as the aircraft cruised through the lower atmosphere. Opponents claimed this had the potential to not only disturb the public but even cause damage to buildings.

Such concerns in the context of civil aviation were in contrast to an earlier US military approach to the problem. To allay public concerns as the likes of the Hustler supersonic bomber disturbed the peace as it cracked sonic booms over the landscape, the US Air Force launched a nationwide campaign promoting it as the 'Sound of Freedom'!

Even after the US finally cancelled its own supersonic transport aspirations in 1971, largely due to economic and noise considerations, the British continued to strongly encourage

Qantas to exercise the four options it had taken out on the Concorde. At one point, they invited captain Alan Terrell, later to be appointed the airline's director of flight operations, to evaluate the aircraft on a test flight out of the British Aircraft Corporation (BAC) centre in Bristol. BAC had scheduled two flights for Terrell, the first on 20 November 1971, and the second three or four days later. During that time, Terrell's position would shift from delight to frustration.

Scheduled between his flights was a similar evaluation flight by Pan American, which also had options on several Concordes. The situation went awry when, halfway through his evaluation flight and to the horror of the BAC test crew, the Pan Am pilot suddenly heaved the aircraft into a steep turn, immediately running the risk of massively overstressing its airframe.

Sitting behind as an observer, Terrell watched as BAC's chief test pilot Brian Trubshaw announced that he was taking control and immediately levelled the aircraft, at the same time shouting to the American: 'Get out of my cockpit! I never want to see you again.' With the Concorde grounded while stress tests were carried out, it was six months before Terrell could complete his second flight.

With Qantas almost completely engaged in its 747 program, it was not an easy task for the British to get the airline to concentrate on the SST. In a last-ditch attempt to convince Qantas to become 'an around-the-world supersonic airline', Trubshaw and a BAC team made Concorde's first visit to Australia in June 1972.

With its spectacular nose-high landing configuration giving the impression of a massive bird of prey, Concorde stopped the traffic on General Holmes Drive as thousands watched it touch down at Mascot. It was the start of an intense several weeks of media interest and demonstration flights.

With aircraft noise by now a controversial issue, the Department of Civil Aviation took the opportunity to assess the Concorde's environmental Achilles heel—the sonic boom. Positioning a ground-based noise-monitoring team at Hamilton Downs station near Alice Springs, it set out to record the sonic boom as the Concorde passed overhead on a flight between Melbourne and Darwin.

Thanks to an accompanying commercial television crew recording the event, the Hamilton Downs mission would have its slightly bizarre side. No one, of course, knew quite how much noise the sonic boom would create as the vapour trail of the Concorde streaked across the sky from the south, so the television news crew decided to focus their camera on the reaction of two crows sitting on a nearby fence. When the muffled crack of the sonic boom from 30,000 feet finally reached the brace of sound monitors strategically placed on the earth, the two crows hardly moved on their perch, prompting one wag to comment, 'I hope these noise monitors will give us a bit more information than the crows!'

In the final analysis, however, the aircraft's impact on the environment would have little to do with the eventual Qantas decision to cancel its Concorde options. The Australian airline's studies had revealed its limited passenger payload and range would prevent it from carrying a profitable load even between Sydney and Singapore without refuelling.

However, as an early airline venture into the supersonic age, there's little doubt the Concorde can still be regarded as a remarkable technological achievement. Although only twenty were produced, it operated for more than 30 years, primarily as a British Airways and Air France flag carrier between London, Paris and New York. During that time it suffered only one major accident. In July 2000, an Air France Concorde ran over debris left on a Paris runway by an earlier aircraft taking off. Part of the debris picked up by the undercarriage wheels fractured the fuel tank, causing the aircraft to burst into flames and crash shortly after take-off, killing all on board.

3
'IT'S BOEING'

When Qantas accepted Boeing's proposal for four 747s, it came at a cost of around A$18.5 million for each plane, included in a company-cost package of $134 million for spare engines, hangar construction, ground support and training aids. Qantas would become the first airline in the world to order and operate the 747B version.

The deal would also lead to more than 40 years of Qantas on-site presence at Boeing's Everett factory outside Seattle, beginning in July 1971. Senior technical representative Ken Gould and his deputy Mick Ryan were the first Qantas staff posted there to oversee their specific production requirements for those first four aircraft, which would roll off the assembly line over the next five months.

There was not much to see when they arrived, as Gould would later note. 'The interesting thing about the 747 was the fact that all of Boeing's customers for the new aircraft, including Qantas, had bought paper aeroplanes. There was no prototype at the time initial orders for the 747 had been placed.'

'Basically, what an airline had in those early days was a shell into which they would feed their own specific requirements,' recalls Mick Ryan, describing the process as 'akin to purchasing a car from the basic model, to which you added roof racks and a tow bar'. In Qantas's case, that 'roof rack and tow bar' customisation would vary quite markedly from that chosen by other airlines.

For instance, in contrast to Pan American, who initially purchased the aeroplane pretty much as Boeing produced it, Qantas's primary aim was to build in as many engineering options as possible, a policy that would pay dividends in the future.

'In the end Pan Am were eventually forced to implement some of the changes as well,' says Ryan.

One example was the installation of an underfloor galley in the cargo hold for food preparation. Freeing up more space on the main deck would not only enable seating for fourteen additional passengers, but it also allowed catering requirements to be taken on board without interfering with the loading of such large passengers numbers—or, for that matter, disturbing passengers remaining on board during transit stops. Only two other carriers, United and American Airlines, followed Qantas's lead.

There was, however, one occasion in the late 1980s when the innovation of a galley in the lower hold had tragic consequences. The procedure was for meals prepared in the lower lobe galley (LLG) to be placed on a trolley and taken by a lift up to the main deck for the meal service. Once the aircraft had arrived at a transit port and its passengers had disembarked, employees from the contracted catering company would come aboard to remove the used food trays and replace them with new ones for the next flight sector.

Safety manager Ken Lewis still has vivid memories of what took place at one such changeover at Honolulu, where the unique Qantas LLG arrangement was the only one of its type serviced by the local airport catering company. With the lift in the 'down' position, the procedure was for the catering staff member in the LLG to place the used meal trays in the lift and send them up to a second catering staffer waiting to receive them on the main deck.

Why the staffer on the main deck opened the door and stepped onto the top of the lift shortly before his colleague below set the lift in motion will never be known. As the lift rose, it crushed him at the top of the lift. His death led to the positioning of a series of triangular fittings atop the lift, making it impossible to enter while the lift was in the 'down' position.

Undeterred by his airline's nervousness, Lewis went against legal advice and decided to attend the worker's funeral on Hawaii's Big Island. 'His family met me with warm arms and we shared a common grief,' Lewis remembers. He also paid for the wake, only to have his subsequent expense claim rejected on the basis it 'might acknowledge Qantas liability'.

Another initiative pressed on Boeing by Qantas, and one that was obvious from both outside and inside the aircraft, was an extension of the upper-deck lounge, increasing the number of windows from the standard three to ten each side. Similar to the stylish first-class cabin beneath it, the upper deck itself would ultimately lead to competition between airlines to experiment with more exotic tastes. In Qantas's case, the area became the Captain Cook Lounge, an explorer-themed escape for first-class passengers to relax or read newspapers. At one point, it prompted Pan Am president Juan Trippe to make a special trip to Honolulu to inspect the Qantas lounge, before he decided to create an exclusive dining area for Pan Am. Once the tables were set and the starched white napery was in place, Pan Am's first-class passengers would be invited upstairs to dine.

Qantas's own Captain Cook Lounge wouldn't last long, with Bert Ritchie once describing it as 'the most expensive piece of real estate in the world'. It was soon converted to passenger seats.

**

One of the most important safety innovations of the jumbo era was another first for Qantas: the development of the inflatable slide/raft for use in the event of a crash on water. Early jet aircraft like the Boeing 707 and the Douglas DC-8 had life rafts stored in overhead locations, which had to be taken down by either passengers or crew and launched out through the door of the aircraft. But the 747 would present a new challenge: how could the hundreds of passengers on the new aircraft be evacuated within a very short period of time?

An invention by Qantas operations safety superintendent Jack Grant came to their rescue, combining the escape slide and the raft into one inflatable item—an emergency evacuation concept which became accepted by aviation authorities around the world. Grant was eventually awarded the Cumberbatch Trophy by the Honourable Company of Air Pilots for his invention.

***

In those early years at the Everett factory, Ken Gould and Mick Ryan hosted a steady stream of Qantas personnel from across the company. Meetings with Boeing officials were often lengthy as the company kept pace with Qantas's specific requirements, both on operational matters and the fitting out of the aircraft.

During these visits, Gould and Ryan would arrange appointments for Qantas officials to see the various mock-up interior designs that Boeing was offering, from which the airlines could choose their individual requirements. It was a task that occasionally had its humorous moments, particularly when in the company of people like Bob Walker. Ryan recalls once taking Walker to see a mock-up in which the very front of the first-class section was decked out in tucked curtains, dimmed red lights and candles, all providing a somewhat seductive atmosphere.

Walker took one look at it, muttered something about it looking like an altar, then, to the surprise of his Boeing hosts, promptly genuflected while making the sign of the cross.

(Walker's response, however, could be considered conservative when compared to that of a US airline chief executive, who took one look and immediately likened the lounge to a 'Hamburg brothel'. As Boeing's Charles Reynolds recalls, no one at Boeing was prepared to take the risk of asking him what experience he had to compare the two.)

Yet another lighter moment came when Qantas suggested it might look at using a section of the lower lobe beneath the main floor as a cabin crew rest area. Boeing subsequently had it so attractively fitted out that one visiting Qantas senior executive was heard to comment: 'That looks so good they'll have to fill it with water to get them out!' But the idea was soon sacrificed on the altar of industrial relations when cabin crew rejected the concept.

Gould and Ryan were the first of many technical representatives to be based in Seattle as the various versions of the 747 ordered by Qantas came off the assembly line, from those early -200Bs of the 1970s, through to the last of the -400s more than 30 years later. The years would also bring significant changes in work practices for those who represented the airline in Seattle.

In Ryan's early days, most of the communication between the customer in Sydney and Boeing was by telephone or telex. Then, according to Ryan, came the first agonisingly slow and cumbersome early fax machines. By the time one of Ryan's successors, Scott Collins, arrived in the early 1990s to serve two years and sign off on ten aircraft deliveries, hard-copy exchanges were a thing of the past. Communication methods had improved dramatically, and they continued to do so through the 2000s with the introduction of such facilities as Webex and the ability to communicate with multiple attendees.

'These days [of the 787s], there are only a half a dozen documents, including the bill of sale and aircraft receipt, still signed in Seattle at delivery,' says Collins. With a tinge of regret, he adds: 'Unfortunately this means the requirement for the senior tech rep to be physically in Seattle has reduced significantly!'

But back in the 1970s, as those first four Qantas 747s began to take shape at the Everett facility, the Qantas Jet Base at Mascot was undergoing a radical—and expensive—expansion of its facilities to handle them.

4
THE JET BASE

For Qantas, it was soon obvious that anything related to the 747 would require a program of unprecedented size. Set-up costs for four aircraft and basic support totalled around A$170 million, with the Jet Base building program alone approaching $30 million.

Included would be a new hangar capable of taking a stretched 747, with an annex to handle airframe component repair, along with extensions to the overhaul workshop for the much larger JT9D engine and its components, a new jet engine test cell, a flight kitchen, a training building, and an advanced flight simulator. Since much of the expansion couldn't be accommodated within the existing Jet Base complex at Mascot, the company purchased 72,800 square metres of land across Qantas Drive.

Along with it came a whole new concept in warehousing spares and other equipment: the establishment of a state-of-the-art stacker/retriever in the airline's Central Store, with a punch-card system that controlled special cranes for automatically selecting stock. Such advancements, combined with the Jet Base's renowned engineering reputation, would see the base endorsed within a few years by Boeing as the only facility in the world authorised to carry out aircraft modification on 747s outside its own plants in Seattle.

Even the normal process of moving more than 300-tonne 747s from the Qantas Jet Base across the north–south runway to the international terminal at the far side of the airport would see yet another innovation. The Fox Tug, a low-profile vehicle to be attached to the 747's nose wheel, could tow the aircraft at 16 kilometres per hour to its terminal gate. Its design allowed the steering wheel and instrument panel to swivel 180 degrees, enabling the Fox to push or pull the 747 in whichever direction the driver intended.

To handle cargo came container-pallet loaders, scissor-lift platforms for lifting the cargo up to deck level, and new, fully enclosed passenger loading steps designed to protect passengers from the elements when aircraft were forced to used remote parking positions. But it would be the 'cherry pickers', as they became known—19-metre-high aerial work platforms used to carry out servicing and maintenance—that would impress people like David Forsyth, who joined the engineering department in January 1970.

'You could stand on the tarmac and reach most of the servicing points on the 707, but not on the 747. Now you needed a ladder, an elevated platform or the cherry picker,' he recalls. And just to help bring home to engineering crews what to expect when it came to the 747's size, Forsyth remembers the company even went to the extent of painting the aircraft's outline on the concrete outside the hangar.

For the Qantas workforce, shift adjustments to gear up for the 747 meant the creation of a night roster in 1970. This brought the Jet Base into a 24-hours-a-day, 7-days-a-week shift pattern to enable the aircraft to return to service much faster than its 707 predecessor.

***

As air crew familiarised themselves with the 747 simulator, cabin crew went into training to handle more than twice the passengers they had ever had to contend with in the past. Denis Simond had been with Qantas for barely a year when the airline placed its initial order for its four Boeing 747s in 1967. Within three years, as cabin crew training manager, he became deeply involved in onboard preparations for the jumbo. As the 747 delivery dates approached, his role expanded to cabin crew recruitment and training, and developing in-flight procedures and standards.

Preparing for the 747s' arrival required a completely new cabin crew training facility, which included the construction of a complete cabin mock-up. At the time it was the most expensive non-operational training facility in Qantas's history, and one which created a template for other airlines to follow. After inspecting the mock-up, officials from

Singapore Airlines, one of Qantas's major competitors, even took the plans back to Singapore to design their own. Yet while many within the company appeared impressed by the authenticity of the training mock-up, few were aware of the clandestine methods Simond and his people had used to achieve it.

Unlike the open overhead racks of its 707 predecessor, the 747 came with large closable lockers. But in those early production days neither the lockers, nor any templates to create them, were available. So, to ensure authenticity in training, Simond discreetly gained permission from his Boeing counterparts in Seattle to unscrew an overhead locker, complete with special valved hinges, as well as a mock-up of an interior door.

'Over several days I had them carried out of the Boeing complex wrapped in brown paper while giving the guards the "everything's okay" salute. It's hard now to imagine the sight of a massive 747 door being carried out through security but the brown paper did the trick, and we were able to copy them for our own 747 training replica!'

Meanwhile, out on the airline's routes, another problem started to arise. Qantas crews began to report they were picking up rumours and negative comments from other airline crews about the 'difficulties' that the 747 was expected to bring, with its 'unknowns' and sheer size, when compared to its 707 predecessor. To counter this, the airline formed a liaison team of twelve flight stewards tasked with briefing the operating crews on normal 707 flights and at slip ports throughout the route. Ultimately, these twelve would be among the first seventeen flight service directors, a new position title that reflected the large numbers of staff required to manage the many different in-flight services the 747 was to offer its passengers. Most of them had never even seen a 747 when they were recruited.

5
READY TO FLY

While various Qantas specialist teams would pass through Seattle as those first four aircraft took shape, one in particular would begin a semi-permanent presence that would be destined to continue for some years into the 747 delivery program. Known as the technical development group, it comprised a small band of pilots and flight engineers who oversaw the more specific operational specifications for the new aircraft. It was a unique set-up among Boeing's relationships with airlines, and the team would play a unique part.

One of the first to be assigned to this group was a pilot who had joined Qantas after RAAF service in World War II. Fred Fox had cut his Qantas teeth on Catalina flying boats in the challenging skies over Papua New Guinea before transitioning to the Boeing 707 and then the jumbo. He began his 747 training on Boeing's own flight simulator in June 1971 before undertaking his conversion training on Qantas's first

Boeing VH-EBA at Seattle two months later. Fox and his acceptance colleague, captain Bert Yates, would soon notch up another notable experience. While doing 'touch and goes' on the second aircraft (VH-EBB) (in aviation parlance, a 'touch and go' means brushing the runway with the wheels before opening the throttles to become airborne again), one engine failed on take-off. It was a first for a Qantas 747.

'When we pushed all the engines up to take-off power, engine number 3 had an exhaust gas temperature runaway and we had to shut it down. I'd never seen a gauge run so fast—you couldn't even see the needle going around!' he remembers. 'There were no problems as the aircraft was not being operated at a very heavy weight, so it performed beautifully and we even completed the circuit on two engines.'

Later tests revealed the engine had suffered no real damage, and VH-EBB was able to leave on its delivery flight several days later. It was, however, an early indication of the problems that would surface with the Pratt & Whitney JT9D engines in those early days.

***

Engine failures aside, Fred Fox soon found that the workload on the acceptance flights on these larger aircraft required the two pilots to be fully engaged—one pilot flying and the other following the acceptance program, recording the performance data and how the aircraft behaved through the check sequence.

Other innovations that came with the 747 were the aircraft's two independent autopilots, a flight director system, and an auto-land capability to make landings in poor visibility—a feature that Australia's Department of Civil Aviation (DCA) initially only allowed for use as a development system until it was further improved. Thus Fox would find himself still involved several years later in more auto-land demonstrations in Australia to allow the DCA to certify the system for use on normal Qantas route flying.

With Bert Yates's retirement, Fox was joined by pilot-development chief Laurie Clark until eventually Fox himself moved on. His successor, captain Alan Bones, had come out of the general aviation industry as an aero club instructor. After studying aeronautical engineering at university, Bones joined Qantas in 1963 as a second officer on Lockheed Electras, gained his flight navigator's licence, then became a senior check captain on 707s.

The final acceptance process for a Boeing 747 followed a fairly standard procedure. Once the aeroplane was completed, Boeing would undertake all the initial ground checks. The plane would then be taken out to the Everett flight line, where the Boeing production test pilots would take it into the air for the first time on what was known as the 'B1' flight. If all went according to plan, the aircraft would remain on the grounds for several days while further ground checks were carried out. Finally, it would be handed over to the Qantas team.

Even though Boeing still owned the aircraft at this point, Clark and Bones would put it through its paces: shutting down engines, and testing hydraulic and emergency systems, and executing rejected take-offs. These rejected take-offs involved bringing the aircraft to a stop part of the way down the runway—in fairly spectacularly fashion, especially to those watching on the ground.

Some of the more extreme routines on these Qantas test flights on the early 747s, which tested the aircraft's flying characteristics, were not particularly popular with Boeing but were required by the Department of Civil Aviation before an aircraft could be certified as airworthy. Bones would later describe the pattern:

> After take-off you would check all the different modes and, as we climbed out, we would be making sure the instrumentation was working perfectly, do some engine handling and then undertake pressurisation tests, actually depressurising the aircraft to make sure all the masks dropped.
>
> Then we would climb to around 30,000 feet, and shut down and relight the engines one at a time to make sure they worked properly. Once that was done we'd shut down half the aircraft's hydraulic control system just to ensure if you lost two hydraulic systems the aircraft was going to fly alright.
>
> Then came the stall test where the aircraft was slowed down to the edge of the stall, prompting buffeting and activating stall-warning alarms. You're just trying to make sure that the guys up there flying it in a year's time know that everything is going to work as it should.

Then they would turn towards the airfield at Moses Lake, east of Seattle, where they would set the aircraft up for an automatic landing approach—a 'touch and go'. Once back on the ground at Seattle, one of the most severe of the ground tests would take place: the rejected take-off, which was certainly not an experience for the faint hearted.

The Boeing 747 had an inbuilt 'rejected take-off system', which was required to be 'armed' before take-off so that if the pilots decided they had to abandon the take-off itself, all they had to do was close the throttles and the auto-braking system would be automatically activated. This was necessarily timed as the final exercise for the day, as 300-odd tonnes of aircraft lurching to a shuddering halt within a short distance created massive heat on its brakes.

Back in the office, the Boeing–Qantas team would work through any problems they had found and decide whether they needed to fly the aircraft again. 'No one really wanted to do that unless it was absolutely necessary as such things cost a lot of money,' says Alan Bones. 'They're Boeing costs at this stage, of course, but as their contracts people would say: "Don't worry, it all goes on the costs of the aeroplane!"'

***

Much-improved technology on the later -400 series of the 747, and on the 767, made many of these early test requirements specific to Qantas unnecessary, to the obvious delight of Boeing. There were, however, occasional exceptions. Bones, who flew acceptance tests on both types, recalls flying a new 767 six times before they finally worked through the problems occurring with some of the flap settings.

Once an aircraft was accepted, there would be a 'round-table' with the various members of the Qantas finance team, and the lawyers and bankers involved in the financial aspects of the aircraft's purchase. Next, they would all climb aboard for the final act: a flight 200 miles (320 kilometres) beyond US airspace and into the North Pacific designed to avoid any taxation implications for Boeing. It was at that point, in the middle of nowhere, that the aircraft would be signed over to Qantas.

Such was the relationship built up between the two organisations that Bones and other members of his technical development group would often be asked by Boeing's own crews to join them on test and acceptance flights on other airlines' aircraft to offer a 'second opinion' if needed.

It must be remembered that the Boeing 747's arrival onto the Australian aviation scene was not solely a Qantas story. Many other factors needed to fall into place before the 747 could take its place in Australia's aviation system. Successful commercial aviation doesn't work without the required ground infrastructure, such as the runways and taxiways capable of handling its various demands. In the case of the 747, terminals needed to cope with an aircraft of more than double the passenger load of its predecessors. This required a heavy commitment from government.

In an article in Australia's *Aircraft* magazine several years before the first Qantas 747 rolled off the assembly line at Boeing, the Department of Civil Aviation's airport and ground facilities supremo Dr Bill Bradfield had no illusions about the challenges ahead. 'It's apparent that the world's airport system generally is not ready for the Boeing 747 and much of this situation is due to insufficient systems planning,' he noted.

Bradfield went on to suggest it wasn't just a matter of increased length and strength of runways. It was also important to widen taxiways to ensure the undercarriage wheels didn't slip off the pavement edges and bog on the grass, and fillets to prevent the blast from the outer engines of the 747 ripping out the runway lights. Even the airport fire tenders then in use would need to be replaced by larger versions capable of throwing foam sufficiently far to blanket the whole of the 747's fuselage, and the fire stations to house them would need to be extended.

Indeed, as it would turn out, the area of Bradfield's responsibility would be where Qantas, diplomatic relationships, politics and even at times the media would meet head-on. The first battleground would be over the terminal buildings to handle the new planes, where not only millions of dollars were at stake but reputations as well.

6
A TALE OF TWO CITIES

Dealing with federal and state governments, along with the demands of the aviation industry and the public, often meant that Bill Bradfield's boss Donald George Anderson needed to walk a political tightrope. As director-general of civil aviation, Anderson's area of responsibility covered a broad swathe of Australia's aviation industry: from politically sensitive negotiations with world governments over Qantas's international traffic rights, to overseeing the regulatory requirements of Australia's domestic airlines, general aviation and light aircraft operations.

There were those who suspected Anderson might have found the inevitable partisan struggles of international negotiations a welcome relief from the domestic aviation part of his role. Australia's vast distances between centres of population have traditionally given airports and their perceived economic advantages much more importance in Australia than in many other developed nations. European nations, for example, have rapid and efficient railways to provide a large part of their transport.

But in Australia, the most controversial planning decisions often involved the air transport system's ground facilities, particularly its airports. If there is one aspect of Australia's civil aviation infrastructure that can be relied upon to create a mix of political mayhem, jealousy and rancorous state rivalry, it's the combination of aeroplanes and the airports they use.

State governments had long been rivals for the general transport and tourism advantages that airports could bring to their own states. There is no better example than the rivalry that surfaced between Sydney and Melbourne when plans were announced to build a new $50 million international airport for Melbourne at Tullamarine. A brand-new Tullamarine was immediately seen as a direct challenge to Sydney's Mascot as Australia's primary international gateway. It was therefore inevitable that the looming demands of the approach of the Boeing 747 would be caught up in the politics of it all as well.

Although there was little doubt that Melbourne had outgrown its Essendon airport, and the forecasted demand for international air services meant that another international gateway was needed on Australia's eastern seaboard, powerful forces in Sydney, among them Sir Frank Packer's Sydney-centric Australian Consolidated Press, were having none of it. Even when the federal government, hoping for an appeasement, agreed to construct a new Sydney international terminal at Mascot in 1970, to be built in parallel with the completion of Tullamarine, they were not placated. Mascot did urgently require a new international terminal, but much of the city-based parochialism in Sydney was generated by the belief that a Melbourne-based Department of Civil Aviation head-quarters would automatically favour Victorian projects when it came to any major airport development.

Thus began a torrid campaign to highlight the contrasts between a brand-new Tullamarine and a further 'patch-up' of Sydney's Mascot. Occasionally the attacks became personal, including when Sydney's *Daily Telegraph* featured an editorial accusing Bill Bradfield of 'being a traitor to Sydney'. Not that Frank Packer was content to restrict the campaign to his print media. On one occasion he assigned his star Channel 9 television personality Tony Charlton to produce a program highlighting the alleged 'bias' of the DCA when it came to favouring Melbourne's Tullamarine over Sydney.

Although Tullamarine's new terminal was still far from completed, the 52-square-kilometre airport site already had in place enough television pictorial opportunities, such as a distinctive state-of-the-art air traffic control tower and an almost-completed main runway, to visually highlight for a television audience the extent to which Tullamarine's development was surpassing Sydney's Mascot.

When the request from Charlton's producer for access to Tullamarine landed on Donald Anderson's desk, those around him were resigned to the inevitability of the contrasting 'visuals' of the two airports to come. So they were surprised when Anderson ordered them to 'open all the doors to any access he wants'. It turned out to be a masterstroke. Not only were Charlton and his team surprised to be given the opportunity for a series of wide-ranging interviews with Anderson and some of his key personnel, but they were offered an open door to any assistance they required for several days of filming the work in progress at Tullamarine.

And when the show subsequently went to air in GTV9's Saturday-night prime-time slot, it was the DCA's turn to be surprised. True to his profession, Charlton presented a balanced report of the Tullamarine story until, midway through the program, it was pulled off air and the station suddenly switched to a sporting event. It was later reported that an angry Packer, watching from home, had been so upset at the even-handed treatment by the show that he called his station and demanded it be taken off air.

As it transpired, Sydney's new international terminal and Melbourne's new international airport would both open in tandem in 1970, just over twelve months before the arrival of the first Qantas 747. In Melbourne, international and domestic terminals were under one roof, but in Sydney they were separated. The reluctance of domestic airlines like Ansett to help meet the cost of the Sydney terminal project would condemn the city's passengers to years of inconvenience, with international and domestic airlines on opposite sides of the airport.

Probably the only other hiccup for the DCA were the words of prime minister John Gorton as he opened the new Melbourne airport. The DCA had for decades stood firmly by a policy of insisting that major Australian airports were not to be identified by their suburban location but by the cities they served. Yet Gorton cut the ribbon with the words: 'To this airport, and the lovely liquid name "Tullamarine".' Like the widely used description of 'Mascot' in Sydney's case, it was a battle the DCA would never win.

***

As for the demands of the 747: with initial planning dating back to the 707 days, substantial changes had to be implemented to ensure that the terminal 'fingers' were lifted to the height required to handle the jumbo. Added to that was the requirement for extensive widening of runways and taxiways to accommodate the length of the 747's wings and the engines that hung beneath.

Despite continuing media criticism during construction, Anderson, his airport guru Bill Bradfield and the Department of Works had everything more or less in place, at least in Sydney, by early 1970. They were just in time. But for Donald Anderson, a more critical assignment would confront him and Qantas when it came to agreeing on where the 747 would be permitted to fly.

As for the pilots who would actually fly the 747s: they had to adapt to massive change while still protecting the company's safety culture.

7
THE FIRST OF BOEING 747 TOUCHES DOWN

The big moment for Qantas arrived early on the morning of 15 August 1971, when the two Qantas HS-125 corporate training jets met VH-EBA *City of Canberra* off the east coast of Australia and escorted it through a formation flypast over Sydney to land at Mascot.

Those sixteen undercarriage wheels hitting the Mascot runway would mark the beginning of a new era for Qantas. It would see the use of seven 747 variants over the coming years, from the -200B version landing that day, through the -300s to several 200 Combi freighters and two long-range SPs (Special Performance versions), and all the way to the 747-400s, 25 of them, from August 1989.

Driving them would be three engine types, moving first from Pratt & Whitney to Rolls-Royce and then to General Electric. A range of different colour schemes and livery would appear, and an assortment of first-class, business-class and economy seat configurations, often depending on the market demands of the particular route flown.

Its arrival at the terminal building that morning would also bring into sharp relief the varying backgrounds, ambitions and personalities of those in the official welcoming party.

Fussing about prime minister William 'Billy' McMahon and his wife Sonia was a brace of federal and state politicians, Qantas board members and airport executives, all anxious to make the most of an opportunity to benefit from the airline's initial step into its wide-bodied future. Indeed the irony of it all could hardly have been lost on some of those in attendance as the minister for civil aviation, Robert 'Bob' Cotton, stood alongside McMahon at the reception. Cotton had been a close confidant of John Gorton, the man McMahon had ousted as prime minister only a few months previously. As the NSW Liberal Party powerbroker who had played a vital role in winning Gorton his prime ministership, Cotton could hardly have relished the company he was keeping.

Leading the Qantas contingent was its chairman Sir Roland Wilson, short of stature but long on experience as a former secretary of the Treasury in the cosseted world of public service mandarins. While Wilson's acumen in the field of economics offered some advantages to the airline, his appointment five years previously, replacing Sir Hudson Fysh, had heralded the start of a series of public service appointments into the commercial organisation. These would, in the years to come, attract frequent criticism, not least from Bert Ritchie, the chief executive standing alongside him.

None of the officials there that day more strongly represented the operational and commercial side of Qantas as it entered the Boeing 747 era than Ritchie. Like many of his colleagues, Ritchie had come out of a war. Flying with Mandated Airlines in 1942—those dark days of World War II—he had evacuated women and children from Rabaul before flying what became known as the 'Biscuit Bombers', ferrying provisions to front-line troops fighting the Japanese on the New Guinea mainland.

After joining Qantas in September 1943, Ritchie converted to Catalina flying boats and became one of captain Bill Crowther's 'originals' who kept the air route to the UK, across the Indian Ocean between Perth and Ceylon (Sri Lanka), open during the war. It was an operation that passed into Australian aviation folklore as 'The Double Sunrise Service': more than 24 hours in the air, much of it through enemy airspace. From Ceylon it was then on to Karachi to link with a BOAC service to the UK. Once the twin-engine Catalinas were replaced, Ritchie continued flying the route in converted four-engine Liberators and Lancastrians, the latter a makeshift civil version of the Lancaster bomber, before eventually moving on to command the first Lockheed Constellation proving flight from Sydney to London in late 1947.

Ritchie would continue to play a dominant operational role leading up to Qantas's decision to enter the jet era with the Boeing 707, and in 1967 he was appointed to succeed Cedric Turner as general manager. A popular GM, he was once described as a 'tough and pragmatic chap who hides under the veneer of the impeccable executive', his silver hair and moustache doubtless adding to the image. After directing the months of frenzied activity necessary to prepare for the airline's first 747, Ritchie must have savoured the glitz and glamour of *City of Canberra*'s arrival as he watched the shiny new jumbo, flanked by the two HS-125s, taxi into the airport's international terminal.

***

In one respect this was a PR masterstroke—an image of contrasts as the airline's two small HS-125 executive jets escorted the first of its giant 747s, *City of Canberra*, into the Sydney International terminal. And it didn't take long for the image to go around the world.

Purchased by the airline in the latter stages of the 1960s, its HS-125s had already played an important role in transitioning pilots from the piston engine cruising speed of 130 knots to the 420 knots of the Boeing 707 jet.

While the 'Pocket Rocket,' as it became known, was used for a variety of purposes, including ferrying crews to Avalon for training on the bigger jets, or for the occasional VIP flight, at weekends it could cross Australia and even venture as far as Port Moresby to log command hours for Qantas captains.

But when it came to taking the HS-125 to Perth it wasn't quite as simple as it looked and fuel consumption had to be closely watched as it fought the headwinds of the westerly jet stream at around 40,000 feet.

That was how, on one occasion, those headwinds led the Qantas HS-125 to come to the rescue of the tiny settlement of Forrest, little more than a 'whistle stop' on the Trans Australian railway near the South Australian border. Forrest boasted an emergency airport in case aircraft ran into problems on the long hop to Perth, although even then the arrival of a westbound Qantas 125 was an unusual sight late one morning when it was forced to land to refuel.

But let's leave it to former Qantas captain Gordon Power to tell the story:

> The local DCA manager met us and after assisting with refuelling we noticed there was some concern on his face when he asked us if we would be making another fuel stop on our return to Sydney the next day, a Sunday. His face took on an even more serious expression when we explained that with the one hundred knot jet stream then behind us we would have no need to refuel on the return flight to Sydney.
>
> He then explained they had a desperate situation. While there is no hotel at Forrest there are venues where alcoholic beverages can be consumed, but they had run out of beer and the next delivery by rail from Perth was some days away.
>
> So the following morning we made a brief stop at Forrest and unloaded several crates of beer.

Many years later Power often wonders how much that extra landing and its exclusive alcoholic delivery cost the airline, which doubtless came out of its training budget.

'But, then again, no one ever questioned what we did on our training exercises. It was all considered to be part of the required experience for Qantas captains. And resolving a serious deficiency in Forrest was just one of them!'

***

Only a few months prior to the maiden 747 flight, Ritchie had been forced to deal with the most serious criminal threat ever faced by the airline: 'The Mr Brown Affair'. Much has been written over the years about the bomb extortion plot that threatened to jeopardise the lives of the crew and 116 passengers aboard a Qantas Boeing 707 en route from Sydney to Hong Kong on 26 May 1971.

'Mr Brown', who would be subsequently identified as 36-year-old Englishman Peter Pasquale Macari, made a series of phone calls to Qantas head office in Chifley Square, Sydney, demanding a $500,000 ransom to reveal where a bomb had been placed on the Qantas Boeing, now well on its way to Hong Kong and, according to Macari, set to explode if the aircraft came below 20,000 feet. To convince the airline and the police the threat was real, Macari directed them to a Mascot airport locker where they found a replica of the bomb Macari claimed he had placed on the aircraft.

While the 707's captain, Bill Selwyn, had crew searching every available space on his Boeing, Ritchie coordinated the efforts of police and the airline's security people, and organised the ransom. In return for $500,000, Macari had said he would reveal the bomb's location and the means of defusing it.

While Selwyn continued to maintain altitude as he turned the 707 back towards Sydney, Ritchie gathered $500,000 in $20 notes from the nearby Reserve Bank, stacked them in two blue suitcases and set off to meet Macari, who would approach Qantas House in Hunter Street in a yellow van. Police were to shadow Macari after he collected the money but their plans went awry when the police assigned to the 'shadow' had difficulty getting a lift in Qantas House. By the time they arrived, Ritchie had already passed over the cash and watched Macari drive away. Shortly afterwards, the extortioner revealed in another phone call to Ritchie that there was no bomb on board the flight.

Federal and NSW police circulated a detailed identikit image of Macari, featuring a moustache and horn-rimmed glasses, while they mounted an extensive search to track him down. One of the few lightly humorous side effects of the incident was the brief detention on several occasions of Bob Cotton's press secretary, who unfortunately bore a striking resemblance to the police identikit image of Macari. On hearing the press secretary had been detained by police on several occasions as he passed through Mascot airport, the Qantas press office couldn't resist sending him a telegram: 'All is forgiven, but please send back the two blue suitcases!'

For his part, captain Bill Selwyn maintained a cool, professional persona throughout the crisis in the air, a factor that played to the airline's advantage in the subsequent avalanche of media coverage.

In January 1972, Macari was sentenced to fifteen years gaol, and after serving nine years was deported back to Britain—ironically, on a Qantas flight. As for the contents of the two blue suitcases, only a little over half of the $500,000 ransom was ever recovered.

But even with The Mr Brown Affair behind it and the first 747 now in situ at the Qantas Jet Base, more hard days lay ahead for Ritchie's airline.

***

In some respects, that first 747 was at the eye of a 'perfect storm'. The arrival of an even bigger aircraft coincided with increasingly bleak passenger forecasts; Middle Eastern countries were driving a massive leap in oil prices; new Northern Hemisphere charter aircraft operators were offering ever-cheaper fares without the cost base of regular carriers like Qantas.

And along with all that came the United States, intent on bullying its way to dominating world air rights and now turning its attention towards Australia and the Pacific, its intent to swamp the route with empty seats. This 'Second Battle for the Pacific', as it would be referred to in the aviation world, would see the US use its big guns—all the way up to the president—to force its own rule of law in air rights, and at the same time teach Australia a lesson.

The confrontation had its genesis in Richard Nixon's administration calling for increased competition, and its Civil Aeronautics Board licensing more operators onto air routes. Some established American carriers, in an effort to cut their resulting losses, responded by 'dumping' seats they now could not fill in the Northern Hemisphere onto routes in the Southern Hemisphere.

The question of air rights between nations has always been a sensitive issue, with respective governments naturally approaching any negotiations with a high degree of self-interest. The post-war years, too, had led to an imbalance in the relative negotiating powers of nations. With the US in ascendancy after the war, it held more power when it came to bargaining in aviation agreements.

At the core of any negotiations was a set of internationally recognised Freedoms of the Air. Several of these covered passenger traffic that could be identified as true origin and destination between the two countries concerned. Still other Freedoms required to be negotiated between countries covered the right to pick up traffic when calling at other countries along a route.

Since the days of the Constellation in the 1950s, Qantas, as Australia's flag carrier, had benefited substantially through such negotiating, particularly the right to operate a prestige around-the-world service from the UK and across the US at a time when such an achievement was a considerable boost to the airline's image. But it too had come at a price: in exchange, the US had the right to carry passengers beyond Australia into Australia's own Asian 'backyard'—rights that would have considerable future value if the US opted to utilise them.

Now, as the 1970s dawned, the US was looking to introduce American Airlines alongside Pan Am as a second flag carrier on the Pacific. By Australia's reckoning, this would make it difficult for any of the carriers to cover their costs, let alone make a profit. The Pacific represented around 25 per cent of Qantas's total traffic, compared to only 4 per cent for US carriers. Those US carriers were offering fares at giveaway prices—in Pan American's case, 80 per cent discounts on fares out of Honolulu to airline and government employees. So, in crude numerical terms, what the US was demanding meant allowing airlines on the route to provide the equivalent of 600,000 available airline seats a year on a route that could barely expect 200,000 passengers.

It was a no-win situation for Qantas. Even much of the Australian media agreed with the US argument that, rather than dealing fairly in a normal quid-pro-quo trade negotiation based on the value to each nation of each passenger's fare, Qantas was in fact standing in the way of cheap fares.

The now-retired Sir Hudson Fysh entered the fray to dispute what he labelled as the unfair treatment of his former airline by the Australian media. In a private note to the company, he lashed out:

Never have I read so much uninformed, inaccurate drivel, avoiding the real issues. Australia is fighting for air transport life against a violently imperial USA brutally trying to crush opposition and immorally fill their planes which they have overbought . . . Will Australian politicians stand up to the challenge or will Australia be subjugated?

While Fysh's outburst might have been a rallying call for Australia to resist the might of America, it once again brought into focus the complex, often brutal world in which the Australian industry itself existed. Beyond such things as safety, equipment choice and competitive customer service, success or otherwise often rested in the hands of others.

When initial pleas for reason fell on deaf ears, Australian authorities at one stage secretly considered denouncing the air services agreement between the two countries altogether. Then the US played its ace card: it finally refused to let the Qantas 747s on the route unless, at least from their viewpoint, a satisfactory agreement was reached. Despite a last-minute attempt at negotiations in Washington, DC, by a team led by Ritchie and Donald Anderson, the US prevailed, eventually winning additional weekly frequencies not only for Pan Am but for newcomer American Airlines as well.

Thus, instead of a US route, it would be the Kangaroo Route to Singapore and London that would see the first scheduled operations of the Qantas 747s—five months before the first jumbo took off for San Francisco in January 1972.

Securing satisfactory air rights would be only one hurdle for the 747 to overcome. The next hurdle—more mechanical problems—would dog the aircraft in the years to come.

8
IT'S ALL ABOUT THE ENGINES

'The JT9D series engine is sick!'

That rather blunt assessment from the Department of Civil Aviation's regional airworthiness engineer John Thorpe sums up the challenges Qantas faced with the early Pratt & Whitney engines that powered the first Boeing 747s. 'In no other transport manufacturing industry is the relationship between the power plant and the vehicle more critical than the aircraft business,' as the late Bob Walker, eminent Qantas engineer, once put it. 'While a harmonious engine/vehicle combination is a logical requirement of all transport modes it is a critical prerequisite to a safe, efficient and reliable aeroplane.'

Walker would also point out that, with their diverse operating requirements, 'one might imagine that the airlines themselves might enjoy an abundance of engine/airframe combinations to choose from: They have not.' Walker's colleague, engineer David Forsyth, would also readily admit

Thorpe's comment was something of an understatement. His own memories of the early Pratt & Whitney engines are of their unreliability and inability to provide the required thrust.

Forsyth, who joined Qantas shortly before the 747s arrived and would later become the airline's engineering chief, admits it was 'sheer luck if an engine lasted twelve months on the wing before something broke. Turbine blades were the most common and when they failed they were accompanied by a vibration, an enormous "bang" and molten metal in the tailpipe.'

Neither were repairs cheap. Each of the 116 turbine blades cost around $1000, not to mention the cost of the resultant damage to other parts of the engine. Then there were the compressor blade failures, usually accompanied by an engine stall, another huge bang and the disconcerting experience for passengers of looking out the window to witness a sheet of flame emerge from the rear of the engine.

Forsyth remembers other component failures causing the engines to shut down, particularly fuel pumps—which, of course, meant no fuel. His list goes on: 'Water injection shut-off valves, thrust reverser motors, bleed air valves and fuel controls all caused lots of problems.'

Not that, as far as Qantas was concerned, aircraft engine problems were anything new. Ever since the immediate post-war years, aircraft engines had been a mixed bag in terms of reliability, particularly with Qantas's uniquely long over-water stage lengths. Some very expensive lessons had been learned along the way. Even the iconic Lockheed Constellation of the 1950s and '60s suffered so many engine failures on the Kangaroo Route to London that exchange engines had to be positioned at critical ports along the route—flown there in the underbelly of one of the airline's specially converted post–World War II Lancastrians.

Right from the 747's earliest days, the engine power needed to enable the jumbo to fulfil its promise and keep it efficiently in the air stretched engine technology to its limits—and, occasionally, beyond. The early Pratt & Whitney was a nightmare: 60 of the 87 engines used during the Boeing testing phase were destroyed. Boeing 747 test pilot Jack Wadell alone experienced 30 engine shutdowns.

And as for the risks involved for Pan Am with its courageous decision to be the launch customer: in one month alone, in 1970, Pan Am experienced 29 engine shutdowns. The airline's engineers must have breathed a sigh of relief when that number dropped to eight shutdowns a few months later. Boeing staff still shudder when they see photographs of those early -100 series Boeing 747s, lined up at the Seattle facility, with cement blocks instead of engines strapped to their wings to maintain their centre of gravity and prevent their tails slamming onto the ground.

Many of the early problems on those first Pan Am aircraft came from 'ovalisation' (see Chapter 1), which caused the high-pressure turbine blades to grind against the sides of the engine, particularly during take-off. Although the problem was eventually resolved, Qantas's Mick Ryan recalls the toll it took on one senior Pratt & Whitney engineer:

'He went from a happy, exuberant fellow to a breakdown and an early grave.'

But more problems were to come in the years ahead, not only with those first Pratt & Whitneys but with subsequent engine marques as well. It took some time for the 747 to acquire an engine that could handle its weight, and in the meantime there were reliability and durability problems, both of which directly affect operating costs, not to mention in-service delays.

And when the boffins came up with remedies, not all of them were popular.

***

Ask any airline pilot what they consider the most critical moment of flight and they will identify the take-off, when all the components of power, speed and lift must come together to propel several hundred tonnes into the air within the limited length of a runway.

To provide the engine boost needed for the 747 on take-off, Pratt & Whitney came up with water injection, a system that pumped thousands of litres of distilled water into the hot sections of the engine when full take-off power was required. The process allowed the cooler air ingested into the engine to keep the turbine area temperatures below its limits and provide additional thrust. In practice, though, it hardly eased the tension for the flight crew during the critical take-off phase, when everything needed to go right.

Many flight engineers and pilots had good cause to

intensely dislike the water-injection system. Facing them was a range of unwelcome possibilities, including an engine failure when the pumps were switched on, one or more engines not receiving water, or the engines running out of water too soon. The process also had a habit of cutting out too early or performing unevenly. If that occurred during take-off, it left the flight engineer with just seconds to make critical thrust adjustments.

Norm King, who rose to be Qantas's chief flight engineer, equates getting a 'wet' take-off right in those days to 'successfully completing a thousand-piece jigsaw puzzle'. Not even practising the procedure during a licence check on the ground-based simulator helped much when it came to the real thing. As King recalls:

In the simulator the 'wet' take-off procedure portion of the check exercise was always done with the aeroplane taxied into position on the runway, lined up and ready for a standing start. The water was switched on and some of the defects the instructor decided to give you to handle were diagnosed before the thrust levers were advanced, or just after you were at less than 80 knots [148 kilometres per hour]—all very comfortable with not much else going on!

By contrast, King describes taking off from the notoriously rough Athens runway, renowned for creating a shuddering control panel, which made it difficult not only to monitor the water injection but to monitor the other instruments measuring engine temperature and pressure ratios. 'It depended as much on the engineer's skill as it did on the reliability of the equipment, and there could be some tense moments,' King confesses. Former captains such as Gordon Power vouch for King's memories. Power remembers one 'wet' take-off from Athens 'which allowed us a very close look at the end of the runway!'

It was not only Athens that presented a problem, as several other former captains attest. Cliff Viertel recalls daunting midnight maximum-weight take-offs from Bombay, bound for London, without much visual reference. While it was an experience 'guaranteed to collectively increase blood pressure in the cockpit, we all accepted it did work', says Viertel, although he recalls some flight engineers jokingly suggested the water was just to 'cool the sensors to make the crew feel better!'

***

While air crew juggled such problems, Qantas engineers were playing their part in helping Boeing solve another issue that was certainly designed to give an operating captain a minor heart flutter: while cruising five or six hours out of Bahrain heading for London, the 747 engine would suddenly increase or decrease power without any input from the pilot.

On investigation, Qantas Engineering found the fault lay with fuel that had been stored in tanks out in Bahrain's heat, enabling a large amount of water to be retained in the fuel.

Once the plane was in flight, that water then froze inside the engine's fuel control unit (FCU). While it was standard procedure for the ground engineers to carry out water-in-fuel checks before any flight, those checks took fuel samples from the cooler bottom of the tanks. Any water in the hot fuel remained undetected.

Even Boeing was initially perplexed, convinced that the movement of the fuel and heating devices in the wings would mean the fuel going into the FCU was above freezing point. So Qantas engineers persuaded them to fit one of the 747s with instruments to measure fuel temperature all along the fuel-flow system. Sure enough, the culprit turned out to be frozen water particles in a shuttle valve in the FCU, which forced the valve to move and caused the engine to either accelerate or decelerate.

Yet another problem encountered with FCUs in those early days was even more serious. On some long sectors, often during descent into Europe, when pilots were required by air traffic control to level out and maintain an altitude, one or more of the engines would not respond and remain at idle thrust. David Forsyth explains: 'On a couple of occasions this affected three of the four engines on the same flight. Just imagine a situation where you can't stop a 747 with a full load of passengers descending into the crowded skies of Europe!'

Power plant engineer John Hocking finally identified that gradual engine wear was affecting its performance, placing extra demands on the FCU as it aged, and he was able to come up with a process by which pilots could prevent or, if necessary, recover from the problem. It reached the point where some pilots were losing confidence in the aircraft, so Hocking held a series of briefing sessions with around 300 of the airline's pilots to help allay their concerns.

Hocking continued to maintain a close liaison with the airline's special development group, which was tasked with looking at such technical issues, whether fuel or fan blade problems. And he continued to liaise with pilots flying the line as well, many of whom expressed deep concern about the engine problems.

Forsyth describes the problems as not only technically challenging but coming during a period of other 'interesting problems, not least regular staff purges and therefore less job security':

Thankfully, back then the airlines and the manufacturers worked closely together to find out what the problems were and to come up with a fix. By comparison, today's aircraft are much more reliable and airlines rarely have to tackle such difficulties, and even if they did, they'd likely be prevented from doing so by modern-day regulatory requirements. And I doubt an airline would be allowed to conduct specially instrumented flights to evaluate fuel temperatures with a plane full of passengers these days!

One engineering and maintenance advantage, however, came with the design of the 747's engines around seven sub-assemblies, or modules, any of which could be readily replaced while the engine was being repaired in the workshop, thus saving much time and expense.

As for engine power: it was simply off the scale compared to the previous generation of fan jet engines used in 707s, which had come with a thrust rating of less than 20,000 pounds-force (89 kilonewtons). By contrast, the engines of the 747 era would grow from 39,000 to 60,000 pounds-force (173 to 266 kilonewtons). Thanks to a combination of continued design improvements, engine management, workshop practices and condition monitoring, their durability on the wing improved from around 2000 hours to over 30,000 hours. 'In calendar terms, that represented a leap from four months to five years,' says Hocking proudly.

Thrust has continued to improve over recent years. Compared to the high point of 60,000 pounds-force (266 kilonewtons) in the case of the four-engined 747, the General Electric GE9X powering today's twin-engine Boeing 777 aircraft is rated at 100,000 pounds-force (44 kilonewtons).

As the first 747 versions spent more time in the skies, a lack of choice when it came to engines would be overcome and while Pratt & Whitney would remain the supplier of engines for the Qantas's first seventeen 747s delivered between 1971 and 1978, Qantas and other airlines would soon be able to take advantage of a bidding war between Pratt & Whitney, Rolls-Royce and General Electric. Eventually the responsibility for the remaining 747-200s and the upgraded 747-300 would fall to Rolls-Royce and their RB211 engine. The RB211 would also power Qantas's two long-range Boeing 747 Special Performance aircraft and, eventually, the Boeing 747-400 that entered the Qantas fleet in August 1989, bringing its own advances in cockpit technology.

9

STORMY SKIES AHEAD— AND NOT JUST WITH THE WEATHER

In the aviation business, there is one single factor beyond the control of an airline that is capable not only of upsetting passengers' plans but of determining an airline's profit or loss on that particular sector.

It's called the weather.

The simple fact is your Boeing 747 can leave a sunny Australia at midday, stop briefly at either Singapore or Bangkok en route, and within twenty or so hours be approaching a London Heathrow airport hidden totally beneath a heavy winter's fog. This, of course, is an age-old problem for aviation, and a series of approach and landing aids have been developed, allowing pilots to descend with limited visibility to an airport using their instrument landing system.

Airport instrument landing systems come in three categories, each dependent upon the equipment on a particular aircraft to read the information transmitted from ground signals.

Categories 1 and 2 permit the pilot to descend 'blind' towards an airport but only to predetermined heights, between 100 and 200 feet (60 metres). If the pilot is still unable to sight the runway, the landing will be aborted, then attempted again—or the flight will be diverted to another airport. Either choice comes at a cost, whether an additional fuel burn for a go-around or, in the case of a diversion to another airport, the more expensive ramifications of passengers missing connecting flights and other schedule disruptions.

The Category 3 provision, however, enables the aircraft's automatic landing system to control the aircraft all the way to touchdown, then roll out to a safe taxi speed. While many airlines, including Qantas, had purchased 747s capable of 'Cat 3' operations, in the mid-1980s alarm bells began to ring in Qantas when the British let it be known that only a small number of 747s would be approved by UK aviation authorities for operation on Cat 3 into London. Any other airline wishing to do so had to provide evidence of their training and procedures before they would be accepted.

With London being such a critical destination on the Qantas network, it wasn't long before one of Qantas's most senior pilots, 747 flight training manager Cliff Viertel, was on his way there for detailed discussions on which aspects of his airline's current operations would need to be upgraded to meet their approval. 'There was no time to argue—just to listen to what they required,' Viertel recalls.

The results were significant changes to the airline simulator training procedures at Qantas's Mascot base, along with a tightening of engineering standards in autopilot serviceability and other aspects. These were quickly upgraded to allow the airline to preserve its winter arrival slots into Heathrow.

For Viertel, however, it didn't stop there. He became deeply involved in drafting new low-visibility approach procedures for pilots, and personally carried out auto-landings on many runways to have the whole Qantas network safety-approved. 'This was all at considerable expense and effort,' Viertel says, 'but the Cat 3 introduction ran smoothly in autumn and winter weather with several approaches at Heathrow and other European airports in visibility as low as 50 metres.'

The end result was another operational first for Qantas. On occasions its flagship flight to London, QF1, would be the only arrival at Terminal 3 during the first foggy hours of operations, providing rapid immigration and customs clearance for the airline's passengers.

***

But such operational successes played out against a background of difficulties confronting the airline at Mascot itself. As the eighties progressed, the increase in fleet size and a shortage of engineers led to a significant portion of Qantas's heavy maintenance program being subcontracted to companies in France, Ireland, the Netherlands and the United States. Viertel describes the resulting situation as 'The Overseas Maintenance Square Dance', with complicated patterns of crew repositioning so that aircraft due for overseas maintenance could be slipped in and out of their normal schedules.

Viertel gives an example of how this worked in practice. A 747 would go in for servicing at Air France's engineering works at Orly airport in Paris. Once Air France had completed maintenance on it, a Qantas flight technical crew would arrive to carry out the required documentation checks and take the aircraft on a test flight over the Bay of Biscay to ensure it was ready to return to service.

Leaving this 747 at Orly, they would then take a passenger flight to Frankfurt in time to meet the regular incoming Qantas flight from Australia the next morning. Once its passengers had disembarked, this plane would be stripped and its galleys cleaned, and the technical crew would fly it to Orly for its own maintenance appointment. There they would exchange it for the already-serviced 747, which they would fly back to Frankfurt in time for its galleys to be refitted and the plane readied for departure that evening on a normal scheduled service to Singapore.

Once the exchange was completed, the technical crew would fly back to London, then head off on a relaxing return as passengers on QF2 to Sydney.

10
'THE PILOTS' AIRLINE'

Of all the people who have made airline history, from the aircraft designers and engineers to the colourful entrepreneurs who financed them, the most recognised are the pilots. It is pilots who have attracted the most public interest, above and beyond the types of aircraft they fly or the engines that propel them. When it comes to the origins of commercial aviation, in the Northern Hemisphere it is the name of Lindberg that people most recognise; in the Southern Hemisphere, it is Kingsford Smith and Ulm.

Move beyond civil into military aviation and you find wartime bomber and fighter pilots who became household names—pilots like Chuck Yeager, who not only carved his initials into World War II, Korea and Vietnam but was the first to break the sound barrier.

Despite the public's perception of its glamour, Yeager had no illusions about his trade. 'There is no such thing as a natural-born pilot,' he once offered, going on to explain that, at least from his viewpoint, 'becoming a proficient pilot was hard work, really a lifetime's learning experience'. That latter comment aptly summed up much of the professional life of an airline pilot.

Even with a lifetime of learning, a pilot could never fly in absolute safety. Decorated RAAF World War II Beaufighter ace 'Torchy' Uren perhaps put this better than anyone. Uren had gained a high public profile in 1943, when a wartime cameraman filmed a newsreel sequence from over his shoulder as he led his 30 Squadron Beaufighters on a low-level attack during the Battle of the Bismarck Sea off New Guinea. Later, as a senior Qantas 707 captain, Uren had no illusions when it came to airline flying, once explaining to members of a pilots' union air safety group: 'We are all interested in safety but if you want 100 per cent safety you are in the wrong business. Safety is compromised when the engines start and the percentage goes downhill from there. We are in the business of flying.'

Many who flew with him would acknowledge, however, that Uren was from an era that was fading with the arrival of the Boeing 747: when pilots were considered a breed apart, even among those who shared the aircraft with them. After lengthy periods in the air and on the ground at 'slip' points along Qantas routes in the days of the 707, Uren was one of many who would rarely be seen enjoying off-duty drinks with anyone outside the circle of pilots, flight engineers and navigators who occupied the cockpit with them. Alan Terrell recalls once suggesting to Uren, after arriving in Honolulu, that they join the cabin crew for a drink later that afternoon. His offer was abruptly declined on the basis that 'they didn't have much in common'.

Another captain from the 747 days tells a story about flying with a few colleagues from Sydney to Avalon airport near Geelong for a regular training checkout. At the controls was Roly Probert, the captain who had delivered Qantas's first Boeing 747. Halfway to Avalon, a first officer was delegated to take cups of tea up to Probert and his operating crew, only to return within minutes with Probert's cup still in his hand. His captain had rejected the offer of the tea with the comment: 'I'm flying.'

When asked why he hadn't left the cuppa there anyway, the first officer replied, 'Would you interrupt Rembrandt while he was creating a masterpiece?' As for some of Probert's colleagues responsible for the training at Avalon, according to yet another captain with memories of those Avalon training days: 'They were a breed apart, straight out of the Captain Bligh School of Public Relations.'

Not that such experiences were limited to Qantas. There are numerous tales of pompous captains on other international airlines, particularly in the immediate post-war years when the Pan American Clippers dominated the skies, and popular movies like *Thirty Seconds over Tokyo* starring Spencer Tracy played to packed houses. Yet another movie of the era, *God Is My Co-Pilot*, starring heartthrob-of-the-day Dennis Morgan, would be quietly renamed *My Pilot Is God* by wags among the post-war breed when it came to categorising a few of their older colleagues.

Humorous asides, however, did not lessen the respect that crews often had for the older captains like Probert, who had a wealth of experience to pass on.

***

While people like chief executive Bert Ritchie, a former pilot himself, would feature prominently in shaping the initial stages of the jumbo era for Qantas, it was one of his World War II compatriots who would set the standards for the airline's enviable operational reputation during the post-war years and into the 747 era.

Like Bert Ritchie, Alan Wharton DSO OBE DFC MID had emerged from World War II, although in a different theatre of war: Ritchie on the Pacific front, assisting in New Guinea's defence against the Japanese, before heading to Perth to pilot Ceylon-bound flights; Wharton via RAF Bomber Command and the fiery skies of Europe and Africa.

Son of a schoolteacher and dux of Lismore High before a brief stint with the Commonwealth Bank, Wharton joined the RAAF at the outbreak of the war in 1939. He won his wings at Narromine, and reached England via further training through the Empire Air Training Scheme in Canada. Posted to the RAF's No. 458 Squadron, at Moreton-in-Marsh in the Cotswolds, he arrived at the station on the same train as the coffins of six pilots who had died in training accidents the previous day. His first assignment the next morning was to act as a pallbearer.

He carried out missions over Germany, delivered bombers to the besieged island of Malta, and took part in bombing raids against the Germans at Tobruk and El Alamein. Returning to England, he completed his second tour over France and Germany. Like many of his era, Wharton rarely spoke of the war, beyond suggesting that his decorations merely meant that he 'was still alive after surviving two tours'.

Home in Australia at the war's end, Wharton joined Qantas flying the crude civil Lancastrians until they were replaced by the new Lockheed Constellations. He stepped out of flying in 1961 to become the airline's director of flight operations, seeing Qantas through the industrially turbulent 707 years where pilot salary negotiations joined the daily operational challenges to make life interesting for anyone in such a quasi-corporate role.

Although with his tall and imposing frame he could easily appear intimidating, Wharton became known for a healthy sense of humour and a ready ability to tell a story against himself. One such story recounts what happened when he learned that Ted Harding, one of his Boeing 707 captains, also owned a fruit and vegetable barrow at Manly wharf. These were the days when pilots' salaries were far lower than they would later become. When Wharton heard that, on his way home from flying duties, Harding had been spotted taking off his Qantas captain's jacket and 'wings' and assisting at the stall, he called him in. 'Ted, I believe you've been seen working in your Qantas uniform on a barrow on Manly wharf?'

When Harding admitted it was true, Wharton then suggested the barrow work didn't present a good image for a Qantas captain and that he should either think about giving up the barrow or leaving Qantas. Harding's reply: 'Boss, can I have a week to think about it?'

On another occasion, when weighed down by paperwork in a period when unpredictable changes in passenger traffic were making it extremely difficult to forecast pilot requirements, he posted a progressive chart on his office wall that read: 'January—too many pilots; February—not enough pilots; March—too many pilots . . .' and so on.

But for Wharton, no such light-hearted banter existed when it came to safety. In his operations division, costs were never an issue for lengthy discussion, even in those times when senior management launched cost-cutting missions across all divisions of the company to compensate for traffic downturns and bare profit margins. Rarely were there any cost compromises in the operations division. Their mantra, 'We do so at our peril,' would gradually morph into a phrase that would identify Qantas for years to come: 'Safety is no accident.'

In an obituary after Wharton's death in 2004, his daughter, Kerri Grant, poignantly wrote of his legacy:

Wharton was with Qantas at a time when flights to London took 60 hours, pilots 'night stopped' mid-flight, messages were sent by Morse code, secretaries sharpened their bosses' pencils and the tea lady came around twice a day. He saw and oversaw many changes and developments but never thought of himself as anything other than a simple man. He was a man of whom Ralph Waldo Emerson might have been thinking when he wrote that the 'mark of wisdom is to see the miraculous in the common'.

Earlier, on his retirement in 1979, Wharton had handed the baton to another popular captain, Alan Terrell, who would dominate the airline's operations for the next decade.

***

When compared to his predecessor, Alan Terrell represented a significant change when he was appointed as the Qantas director of flight operations in 1979. His era represented the severance of the link with World War II, for although there were still air crew who had come through the war years, their ranks were now thinning as pilots with civil, commercial and general aviation experience joined the airline.

Wharton's replacement, as the saying goes, 'came a little out of left field' for Qantas. Born in Darjeeling in 1928, where his father managed a tea plantation, Terrell arrived in Australia with his family in 1946, initially studying engineering at the University of Queensland while his family ran a dairy farm and later a small crops farm alongside Brisbane's Archerfield aerodrome.

Sitting on his Ferguson tractor one morning, Terrell watched a Tiger Moth land on the other side of the aerodrome's wire fence and was surprised when the pilot of the Moth came over and asked him if he'd like to go for a ride. It marked the start of a career that saw him earn a commercial licence and then a job with Australian National Airways in Melbourne.

His first venture into the co-pilot's seat was on one of the airline's Bristol Freighters, ungainly, flat-nosed, twin-engine transports occasionally referred to by some pilots as 'Bristol Frighteners'. Terrell's own description sums them up: 'They were lumbering old things and quite heavy to fly because their bulbous nose was pushing an awful lot of air.'

Graduating to DC-4s and DC-3s, Terrell was introduced briefly to flying British royalty, a function that would feature in his later career. By his own description, though, his initial involvement with Queen Elizabeth and the Duke of Edinburgh during their 1950s visit to Australia was hardly noteworthy. While a Qantas Constellation performed the primary role of carrying the Queen and the Duke, Terrell's ANA DC-3 was to act as a support aircraft, bringing along the royal couple's luggage. In addition to his contribution as co-pilot, Terrell would also manage to put his foot through one of the royal suitcases as he climbed over them to get to the cockpit.

After joining Qantas in 1955, Terrell went through the customary ritual of gaining command hours by flying in New Guinea for several years, on everything from the company's ageing Catalina flying boats to the single-engine de Havilland Beavers and Otters, the latter of which performed so badly in the hot climate of New Guinea that he repeatedly questioned the company's decision to buy them at all. Even when he returned to Australia in late 1960, he was still unable to find anyone in Qantas who would own up to it.

The story of his later captaincy of Boeing 707s and 747s often reads like an aviation version of a *Boy's Own* adventure, from flying the Concorde, the Airbus A310 and A320, and the DC-10, to carrying prime ministers Gough Whitlam and Billy McMahon on numerous official overseas visits.

As well as representing a changing of the guard from World War II to post-war aviators, Terrell was the first director of flight operations at Qantas to retain full flying status, a move designed to maintain firsthand contact with operating crews. In this role, he would provide important guidance for the company in the key decisions of the years ahead, as the iconic 707 began to fade and was replaced by seven different 747 variants. Thus it was first Wharton, then Terrell, who set the operational pathway for the years of the 747 in Qantas service.

Later, as general manager operations, Terrell remained deeply involved in the airline's administrative and operational areas, including to employ the airline's 747 SP in Australia Asia Airlines colours to operate services to Taiwan in 1990, a decision which called for a high degree of political sensitivity when it came to Australia's relations with the People's Republic of China. On his retirement in 1989, after 34 years with the airline, Terrell continued his aviation involvement with the Royal Flying Doctor Service, a relationship he had actively supported during his time at Qantas.

While Wharton's and Terrell's operational leadership would see the airline through the important early years of the 747 in Qantas service, others who held senior positions in the company faced their own challenges, primarily to make this new giant of the skies pay its way towards a profit. Added to that was the fact that government ownership of the airline meant that such a visible Australian icon could never be far from the politics of it all.

11
POLITICS AND MINISTERS

Right from the earliest days of the 747 on the drawing board at Boeing, through the initial Qantas decision to buy it and determining the routes it would fly, the 747 era at Qantas was always intrinsically linked to Canberra and politics. It may seem remote from Boeing's technological achievements or the business of selling a passenger a ticket, but along with every development and decision came the government ministers, board chairs and board members who were required to approve them.

Qantas was, after all, one of the highest profile Australian government organisations of all, and they were the ones who signed off on one of the nation's largest financial guarantees. Whether in politics, business or public service, they were a mixed bunch, and they each brought to the task their own unique style. As seen in politics, such appointments could be something of a revolving door. Ministers would move from one portfolio to another over the life of a government, often resulting in appointees who did not have any identifiable background in the industry for which they had ministerial oversight.

Such was the case with Reginald William Colin Swartz, the first minister of the era leading up to the introduction of the Boeing 747 into Qantas service, and the essential ground facilities and infrastructure it demanded. Entering parliament as the Liberal candidate for Darling Downs in Queensland in 1949, Swartz served as minister for repatriation, for social services, and for health before his appointment as minister for civil aviation in the transition from the Menzies to the Holt government in 1966.

When it came to his public profile, Reg Swartz was a contradiction. While he eschewed the limelight in the House of Representatives, he certainly ensured that the media of the day knew what he was up to, making a name for himself in the parliamentary press gallery, not least via a veritable deluge of press releases. Some of those landing on reporters' desks might have been regarded as having doubtful value. Once, while minister for repatriation, he had announced his department had changed the colour of their repatriation-hospital blankets from blue to grey.

On arriving in the aviation portfolio, Swartz continued his unique policy of releasing at least one press release a week, with the inevitable result that the media occasionally took him to task. On one notable occasion, when he announced the introduction of a commuter air service from Perth to Rottnest

Island, the editorial writer in the *West Australian* not only labelled the release as 'ridiculous' but went on to divide the number of words in it by the meagre number of miles between Perth and Rottnest, finally pointing out: 'That's twenty words a mile!'

His successor as minister, NSW senator Bob Cotton, would pass through a period of much greater challenge and controversy, his earliest days coinciding with Qantas's confrontation with the US government over service rights across the Pacific (see Chapter 7). Cotton's public support for Qantas was a feature of his time as minister, and he took pains to emphasise that while it was the responsibility of the airline's board of directors to remain profitable, they were not alone: 'They can expect me to help them as far as possible to keep financially successful.'

Beyond the sensitive situation on the US route, tensions of another type began to develop on the home front as the 1972 election neared. An advancing Whitlam Labor Party brought signs that several decades of Liberal government rule might be coming to an end. By then, John Gorton had voted himself out of the prime ministership to be replaced by Billy McMahon—no friend of Cotton's, although, like all key ministers, he was called on to support numerous Liberal candidates in their electorates.

One of Cotton's assignments in the lead-up to the election was to support Jim Forbes, then minister for the army, as he campaigned in Mount Gambier in the South Australian electorate of Barker. Booked into a local motel, Cotton and several of his advisers were about to leave for that night's electoral rally when Cotton turned on the ABC TV news, just in time to catch an interview in which McMahon appeared to suggest that he occasionally had to urge some of his ministers to 'work harder'.

Stunned that anyone would air such a criticism of his own team on the eve of an election, and already well aware that the Liberals had an uphill fight on their hands to win against the Whitlam surge, Cotton turned to his private secretary: 'Maybe we should find out what's on at the movies here tonight instead.'

He did, however, honour his commitment to the party at Mount Gambier that evening. But the writing was on the wall and within weeks the McMahon government was consigned to history.

***

The arrival of the Whitlam government amid a brace of 'It's Time' banners in December 1972 brought with it a reformist agenda that was to radically change Australia's political landscape, and with it the nation's aviation industry. In many respects, it would never be the same again.

While a range of newly inducted ministers moved quickly to change the direction of the government departments they had inherited, Charles Keith Jones, a former lord mayor of Newcastle, went much further, gathering all transport arms— from road and rail to shipping and aviation—into a single jurisdiction, a giant portfolio known simply as Transport. In a move particularly significant for Qantas, it meant the long-serving permanent head of the Department of Civil Aviation,

Donald Anderson, would be appointed to replace Roland Wilson as Qantas chairman.

It didn't take those in Qantas long to realise that 'Charlie', as transport minister Jones was commonly known, had a far greater affinity with the land and sea constituencies of his department, and the aviation community found itself struggling to maintain much sense of priority in the general Canberra hierarchy. Indeed, there were times when they watched in awe at Jones's ability to tread, however accidentally, where few other politicians would dare to when it came to matters of aviation.

One of Jones's parliamentary colleagues, Barry Cohen, recalled in his book *Life with Gough* another notable Jones exchange. Early in its term, the Labor cabinet decided, as a public example of self-denial, that all federal MPs would travel economy instead of first class. Jones would have none of it, describing it as 'the most bloody stupid decision this cabinet has made. Ministers are putting in 100 hours a week as it is, and one of the few opportunities we get to work is on the plane. Now we won't even be able to do that in comfort.'

It was an outburst that prompted Whitlam to respond in his own inimitable style: 'I travel economy and I'm a great man and I could travel economy the rest of my life and I'd still be a great man. But most of the people around this table are pissants, and they could travel first class the rest of their lives and they'd still be pissants.'

Charlie Jones's response was not recorded.

***

As for Qantas itself, by the time Jones arrived on the scene the airline's decision to await the longer-range, more powerful B version of the 747 was already making a significant contribution to the airline's bottom line. Its advantages over the airline's remaining Boeing 707s were also brought into stark relief. With one 747 capable of carrying two and a half times a 707's capacity, it was only a matter of time before the last 707 retired.

Soon gone, too, was the Labor government and Charles Keith Jones, crashing down in the Dismissal of December 1975. Regardless of which brand of government was in power, few examples of government 'generosity' matched its ability to appoint the chairman and board members to such a prestigious Australian company.

While such appointments primarily marked Qantas's pre-privatisation era, it would be a scion of that Whitlam Labor government, senator Gareth Evans, who most succinctly summed up the legendary status of appointments: 'The Qantas board is what a government needs when it hasn't got a House of Lords.'

In terms of chairmen, three former public servants would be the first to see in the 747 era: Roland Wilson, Donald Anderson and Lenox Hewitt. All three would bring differing approaches to the role.

Wilson was a somewhat dour character, though with valuable government contacts when it came to the financing of the early 747 purchases. Described as an enigma by those who worked under him, with 'an inhibiting and negative effect on people' both inside and outside the company, he had a style that prompted the airline's public relations staff to attempt to soften his image. There was even a series of favourable profiles in the company's own staff communications.

That such steps were needed must have been obvious to those government leaders and industry elite attending the lavish dinner at Sydney's Wentworth Hotel in November 1970 to mark the airline's 50th anniversary. It was a watershed moment for the airline created by Sir Hudson Fysh and Paul McGinness a half-century before.

Sydney's *Sunday Telegraph*, however, would see it differently, taking Wilson to task a few days later:

> The most mystifying feature of the giant Qantas 50th Anniversary dinner was the apparent brush-off of Sir Hudson Fysh and Sir Cedric Turner. Hudson Fysh was placed almost at the extremity of the huge official table. Sir Cedric was even worse placed. There was a brief mention in the official speeches of these two very remarkable men.

Wilson's seven years as chairman, however, would be marked by five years of profitable growth, and ended several months before the arrival of Qantas's fourth Boeing 747.

Wilson's successor, Donald Anderson, might have had an comprehensive background as a civil aviation administrator, and in leading the international negotiations that helped establish Qantas's international network, but he suffered from the perception within the company that his appointment as chairman had been one of political convenience for Charlie Jones. Still, any criticism of Anderson was partly tempered by an acceptance of his aviation background. Appointed chairman in 1973, his term was to last only two years before he stepped down due to ill health and died a few months later, in November 1975.

Anderson's successor to the Qantas chair, the third consecutive public service appointment, was a former head of the Prime Minister's Department who would leave an indelible mark on the company, particularly on those who were destined to work closely with him.

Cyrus Lenox Simson Hewitt's modus operandi as chairman would be markedly different to that of any of his predecessors. His background as a permanent head in Treasury and the Prime Minister's Department, the latter during the years of the Gorton government, would see him rapidly develop a fearsome reputation for involving himself in the minutiae of Qantas's operations, often on matters that would hardly be expected to occupy much of a chairman's time. A tendency to delve deeply into such areas as the airline's catering arrangements and even the amenities it provided its first-class passengers was one of his most notable features.

International relations manager Tom Roff remembers being called to his chairman's office one afternoon to discuss air rights negotiations with another country, only to find Hewitt and a small group of senior executives discussing the quality of bundles of toilet paper strewn across the table. Roff remembers another of his colleagues being called on to gather hand towels from all international airlines serving Australia so his chairman could compare their quality with those in Qantas first class.

But it was the matter of food on aeroplanes in which Hewitt showed an interest bordering on obsessive. Some might have regarded it as trivial or even a laughing matter, but it had the potential to strike at the careers of those in the line of fire. Jim Bradfield, at one point the executive in charge of customer service, found himself in his chairman's sights over what would become known as 'The Marmalade Saga'.

Hewitt had claimed the jam served was not up to the standard of Qantas first class. So, after first establishing a tasting panel to determine a shortlist, Bradfield launched an Australia-wide marmalade hunt for the best jam he could find to satisfy his chairman's tastes. Heartened when one of his earliest discoveries was a brand that came in cute little jars and could easily fit into the silver-service accoutrements of the first-class meal tray, Bradfield was soon on the line to the woman in Kirribilli who produced it.

'But when I explained I was from Qantas there was a gulp on the other end of the phone and I immediately got the impression it all came from a pot on her kitchen stove!' Bradfield remembers. 'Producing enough to serve the Qantas requirement was out of the question, so that one had to be quickly cut off the list.'

Fortunately, by the time the next best offering on the shortlist was ready to be presented to his chairman, it had dawned on Bradfield that what he should have done in the first instance was to ask Hewitt where *he* considered the best marmalade came from. The answer came back: it was the marmalade served at the Qantas-owned Wentworth Hotel where Hewitt stayed while in Sydney. Bradfield telephoned the hotel's manager to find out the source of their marmalade, only to be taken aback by the answer: 'It's IXL—out of a can.'

Bradfield says he had no problems with jam after that.

For marketing executive Brian Kirkham, working in the airline's Brisbane office, it was the yoghurt.

Hewitt had declared the yoghurt he'd been served on a domestic flight to Brisbane was so good it should be placed on Qantas flights, so Kirkham quickly made contact with the owners of the small family-run yoghurt business in Caboolture. Next came an order from head office for Kirkham to personally head to Caboolture and obtain a sample, chill it, and deliver it to director of marketing George Howling in Sydney. They would then both parade before Hewitt for a tasting session.

Kirkham still remembers sitting nervously with Howling outside Hewitt's open office door and listening as his chairman berated some high official in Canberra over the telephone. Although Kirkham had no idea who was on the other end of the line, he would forever recall Hewitt's final words before hanging up: 'Ministers have lost their portfolio for less.'

Once inside the chairman's office, Kirkham ripped the top off the yoghurt. Hewitt inserted a finger, declared it the best and encouraged them both to get it on Qantas flights as soon as possible. The following morning, Kirkham was back in

Caboolture to present the good news to the yoghurt company's management:

> They felt all their Christmases had come at once, thinking all they had to do was drop the yoghurt off at Brisbane airport. When we pointed out they'd need to get it to all our transit ports around the world, in prime condition and on a daily basis, they nearly died, obviously now thinking of the potential of food poisoning in places like Singapore, Bahrain, Bangkok and Bombay if their delivery system couldn't be guaranteed to work satisfactorily.

The following day, the factory's owners told him they'd decided to decline the offer.

For Len Coulson, it was the ham.

When Coulson arrived to take up his posting as Thailand manager, one of the first items his secretary drew to his attention was 'the ham file', by now several inches thick. Legend had it that this originated when Hewitt, passing through Bangkok on a Qantas flight, had questioned the cut of ham provided to him in first class, so had wrapped a sample in an internal company mail envelope and sent it back to Coulson's predecessor with a note: 'Don't try to tell me this is leg ham.'

Perusing 'the ham file', Coulson discovered that although the onboard first-class menu listed 'hand-carved leg ham', Hewitt had apparently been served cuts off the Bangkok catering centre's slicing machine. Checking with the caterers, Coulson confidently assured Hewitt when his chairman asked on his next transit of Bangkok: 'Greetings Mr Coulson. How's the leg ham?'

Coulson assured Hewitt he was confident he would find it to his liking. 'Unfortunately our Manager Singapore copped it when the chairman landed there. Apparently the caterers had glazed it!'

But it would be the case of whether the French-cut lamb chop served in first class should be served with two bones or one that would have much more serious implications for the company, eventually costing Qantas the services of Henri Leutzinger, the airline's executive chef.

Leutzinger was a man with a worldwide reputation in the development, preparation and presentation of airline food. But while culinary tradition might proclaim two bones as the traditional restaurant dining requirement, he considered such a situation was hardly practical from an airline catering viewpoint. What was the use, he argued, of a superfluous bone on an aeroplane meal if it wasn't going anywhere?

To the sadness of many in the upper echelons of the company, Leutzinger lost the battle that followed. He was subsequently demoted to the catering test kitchen, leading soon after to his resignation and quick employment with a very appreciative Ansett Airlines.

***

Such 'onboard' issues were, to many of those responsible, a by-product of a chairman who, far more than his predecessors, spent much of his time in the air. Hewitt appeared to thrive on representing Qantas at official occasions, from high-level international transport forums to more mundane events such as opening a new Qantas office in a far-flung corner of the world, the latter habit leading to one staff member suggesting they nickname him 'Can-O-Mat', after a popular can opener of the time, on the basis that 'he'd open anything'. And although no one could question his work ethic, even that could lead to the occasional problem for Hewitt himself.

To ensure the necessary files kept pace with Hewitt's frequent overseas travels, his office organised a heavy brown plastic bag to reach him wherever he was in the world. As it turned out, this bag had a tendency to 'go astray' at the hands of some staffer who had a score to settle.

Airport manager John Picken had just arrived at Brisbane airport one summer morning when he bumped into Hewitt in the airport car park. 'It was a hot, muggy day and the chairman appeared dishevelled, soaked with perspiration, his tie loosened and close to exhaustion,' recalls Picken.

'When I asked him why, he replied that he had just flown in from Manila only to find his bag was missing. He therefore insisted on being taken back to the aircraft, a Boeing 707, which of course in the pre-747 days didn't use containers for passenger baggage. So he had gone in and searched the baggage hold himself, obviously without success.'

When Picken broke into a chuckle at the image of the airline's chairman climbing around inside the baggage hold, Hewitt cut him short, suggesting he failed to appreciate Picken's humour and ordering him to contact the Philippines to ensure none of his bags had been left behind. When Picken called the Philippines, he got the answer he expected: it appeared the chairman's bags had been deliberately 'lost' by an aircraft loader.

By early 1980, however, with the end of his five-year tenure approaching and despite his own very public efforts to be reappointed for another five, Hewitt rejected the Fraser government's counteroffer of one year only and resigned.

What is not widely known, however, is that despite his fearsome reputation among the majority of Qantas staff who dealt with him during his time as Chairman Hewitt, there would be those in subsequent years to whom he would show a genuine appreciation, among them former chief executive John Ward:

> Shortly after I left Qantas he made contact and invited my wife Edna and I to dinner at the Australian Club and during a pleasant evening he reminisced about his time at Qantas and how his departure took some time to get over. He was very good company and really very fond of Qantas and some of its people.

Lenox Hewitt died, aged 102, in February 2020.

His replacement as chairman not only ended a succession of public servant appointments, but it heralded a new style of chairman altogether.

***

Mild mannered and softly spoken, James 'Jim' Bolton Leslie would be a sharp contrast to Hewitt in the chairman's role. Even the circumstances surrounding his first contact with the airline as its Qantas chairman in 1979 took many by surprise.

Only just retired from Mobil, Leslie was returning from a holiday overseas with his wife when the government announced his appointment. As was the Qantas custom, the chairman's office alerted the airline's airport manager that their new chairman was due to arrive into Sydney that morning from Honolulu. But with a guitar he had bought for his son slung over his shoulder, Leslie somehow slipped by unnoticed by the airline's airport staff who were lined up to greet him, much to the delight of the aircraft's captain, who jokingly thanked them for welcoming him instead.

It didn't take long for Leslie to develop a close relationship with Keith Hamilton. As chief executive, Hamilton had been near-invisible during the Hewitt years, after realising it would be difficult to share the public stage with such a chairman. Although somewhat publicity-shy, Hamilton was deeply respected by his peers—no one associated with him ever doubted his unparalleled knowledge of the industry and the airline's role in it. Hamilton himself, though, was something of an enigma.

Under Leslie, Hamilton adopted a far greater public role as the face of the airline. His deep knowledge of the industry saw him move more broadly into the international aviation sphere. Thus Leslie, along with many in Qantas, was visibly shaken when Hamilton died suddenly from a massive heart attack at age 56 while gardening at his Sydney home in December 1984. 'With untiring energy he did not spare himself in the Company's service,' Leslie wrote in a note to all Qantas staff.

Determined to avoid delay, Leslie moved quickly to appoint deputy chief executive and chief operating officer Ron Yates as Hamilton's successor, at the same time telling several close to him that he considered Yates, already close to retirement himself, to be a safe interim option to 'steady the ship'.

Eventually, in 1986, Yates's successor was appointed, and for the first time in the airline's history it was an outsider. Former News Limited executive and public service chief John Menadue brought with him an increased focus on exploiting inbound tourism opportunities in Asia and Japan. A deterioration in Menadue's relationship with the board saw him depart the company, amid widespread media coverage, in late 1989. Within months, Jim Leslie would also be gone, replaced by another private enterprise chairman, former chief executive of Ford Australia Bill Dix.

Now, as the airline entered the nineties with 29 aircraft in their well-established fleet of 747s, supported on the shorter routes by twelve 767s, much of the board involvement's in the 747 was largely restricted to signing off on the new 747-400 and 767-300 deliveries over the next three years. In the meantime, it would be up to Dix's successor, former Brambles chief executive Gary Pemberton, to take the airline to privatisation in March 1993, at the same time bringing to a close a lengthy era of government board appointments.

In many respects it was not before time. Any reminder of dealing with board members in the days before Qantas was privatised in 1993 can still elicit wry smiles from those at senior levels in the airline. Some have bitter memories of how such dealings had the potential to ruin careers. Others remember the often-bizarre nature of some of the board requests.

***

In company parlance it became known as 'The Bathing Cap Saga', and it started when Lady Dorothy Antico, wife of board member Sir Tristan, arrived for a break in Fiji to find she'd left her bathing cap back home in Sydney.

The easy solution might have been for her to buy a new one but instead it was 'Drop everything you're doing' in the Qantas company secretary's office, and the Antico family Rolls was despatched from Mosman to Qantas's city office with the cap. From there a Qantas staffer rushed it to Mascot's international terminal, placed it in a new cabin bag in time to catch the next flight to Fiji, where the local Qantas manager cleared it through customs and drove it an hour to the Fijian resort.

Even Sir Tristan himself had his moments, once missing a flight thinking '1645' on the ticket meant 6.45 p.m.

As surprising as it seems, given they were board members of an airline, such scheduling missteps seem to have been a problem for several of Sir Tristan's compatriots over the years. One newly appointed Queensland board member changed a flight from Brisbane to Sydney without informing anyone at Qantas, therefore arriving at Mascot with no transport to meet him. After choosing to walk to Qantas's head office near the airport, the next stop was the chairman's office to inform staff that if this was the way Qantas treated its board members then they could keep the job.

Not that such status sensitivities were the sole province of board members. One senior executive during James Strong's time as chief executive in the nineties arrived at London's Hyde Park Corner hotel to request he be moved to a room of similar size to that booked for one of his senior colleagues. When the Qantas staffer responsible for booking the rooms checked with the hotel, they told him the rooms were all the same size, just different shapes!

And for some unknown reason, being posted to Qantas's New York office held particularly unique risks for Qantas executives. New York manager Peter Picken once arrived at the airport with his driver to collect then-chairman Sir Roland Wilson, only to find that one of his own staff, Joyce Chivers, known to have a close relationship with Wilson, was already there to meet their chairman. To Picken's surprise, as they exited the terminal Wilson asked Picken's driver for the car keys, then drove off with Chivers, leaving Picken and his driver standing on the kerbside.

Wilson and Chivers would subsequently marry in 1975.

Not quite so benign, however, was the experience of another New York manager, Rick Granger. With a prior commitment to an important meeting with the company's legal representatives, Granger delegated his secretary to meet the wife of a board member on her arrival at Kennedy airport.

When the two missed each other at the airport, the board member's wife was forced to share a cab with a male stranger to her hotel.

'When our board member arrived a few days later I apologised and explained what had happened. He seemed to understand and I thought no more about it,' recalls Granger. Word reached him several months later, however, that the board member had complained to the general manager on his return to Sydney and, as a result, and it didn't take Granger long to realise he would never again hold a senior position in the airline.

Faced with such a lack of career prospects, but with an extensive background in the travel industry, Granger took ten days leave in Sydney to look for another job. He resigned, and subsequently established a successful travel business.

On occasions contrasts with other company board members could be stark. Long-time Qantas executive Norm Leek remembers Qantas deciding to hold a board meeting in Auckland during his time as New Zealand manager. Faced with finding enough VIP cars for arriving board members, along with still more for city tours for board members' wives, in desperation Leek asked his opposite number at pipes manufacturer Humes Limited whether he could arrange transport from the airport for the Humes general manager Kenneth Wilkinson, also a Qantas board member.

'No problems, Norm. I'll tell him to grab a cab.'

12
A PILOT'S VIEW

Pilots have always preferred certain types of aircraft, from the very early days of aviation. It's something the general public became aware of in the aftermath of World War II, when former fighter aces began to compare flying a Spitfire to the Messerschmitt 109, or a Curtiss P-40 Kittyhawk to the Japanese Zero. Their favourites were not only dictated by the thrill of flying such machines, but the more important consideration of a particular machine's ability to help keep them alive.

Similar sentiments were transferred to peacetime, and while the workplace of today's airline pilot is a far cry from a wartime fighter's seat, pilots still revere particular types of aircraft. Nowadays it's Boeing and Airbus that are the subject of comparison, and opinions and loyalties often diverge.

'Occasionally one aeroplane catches the imagination of pilots and cabin crew, or even of the general public,' notes

British Airways captain Mark Vanhoenacker, who has written widely on the subject. 'More than a few colleagues have told me they decided to learn to fly only because they wished to fly the 747.' He acknowledges this bond between a pilot and their current aircraft is often hard to pin down, as each aircraft family, like any family, has its own language, or at least its own dialect, meaning that 'analogous devices and procedures often have different names on different aircraft'.

'Emotionally, a pilot's relationship [with an aircraft] is perhaps similar to how some people respond to a prized car they have owned for a decade or two,' says Vanhoenacker, although he acknowledges that 'different cars are not as different to drive as different airliners are to fly'.

When it comes to the long-haul pilot, such relationships involve not only sitting in a relatively confined space, experiencing the vagaries of weather and operational problems that might occur. In the age of terrorism pilots are also essentially cut off from the rest of the aeroplane, even to the point of having their own toilets. Thus, spending much of your life in either an Airbus or a Boeing cockpit can bring out sharp differences and preferences—and, when it comes to aircraft like the 747 or the Airbus A380, even between pilots themselves. These can prompt good-natured quips, such as this one from a former 747 captain: 'Boeing 747 pilots can ENJOY while Airbus "drivers" can only WISH!!'

Retired captain Richard de Crespigny would certainly contest that claim. In November 2010, he successfully brought down his A380, on flight QF32, when one engine exploded shortly after take-off from Singapore. Although he acknowledges the A380 is much more complex, de Crespigny rates its fly-by-wire technology, where computer-regulated flight control systems electronically replace traditional mechanical flight controls, as the best in the industry. Along with that is the A380's range: 'When you compare it with other aircraft it can do seventeen and a half hours Dallas to Sydney, well beyond the range of a jumbo.'

But, like most of his genre, de Crespigny is quick to praise the enviable record of the 747 and what it brought to the industry, acknowledging that in longevity alone it has been in service for almost half of the 118 years since the Wright Brothers' first flight. While he talks in glowing terms of such technological breakthroughs as the Airbus fly-by-wire technology, he is also quick to praise Boeing for its determination to apply aviation's golden rule—to be evolutionary and not revolutionary. 'And that is where Boeing was so successful with the 747. Look at the later problems with the 787 when they tried to be revolutionary with composites, electrics and outsourcing.'

De Crespigny suggests the days of the four-engine airliners are now largely over, given the development of the massive thrust capabilities of the two engines that power the lighter and more streamlined twins like the 777. So are other innovations, like Boeing's 'fifth podding', where a spare engine could be ferried under the wing to replace an engine failure along the route. De Crespigny though, has little doubt about one aspect: 'However you look at it you have to admire what

Boeing achieved with the Boeing 747, and derivatives of it that are still flying today.'

As for transferring from Boeing to Airbus, current Qantas captain Greg Miller describes the transition to the A380 as quite challenging and involving a change of mindset to operate 'the Airbus way', which he admits some of the more senior pilots struggled with. While Boeing tended to allow a degree of latitude in their procedures for what some air crew regarded as 'common sense and airmanship', the A380 came with a very prescriptive set of procedures and it soon became very obvious if you were not following them.

'Thus, adherence to the procedures was heavily advocated and forced home in the simulator and on line checks, making it probably the most standard fleet I have ever operated on,' says Miller. 'It doesn't mean it was the best fleet, as the aircraft was incredibly complex and was always throwing up systemic issues that required a lot of head scratching to solve.'

Looking back, however, Miller regards moving as a first officer from the Boeing 767 to the 747-400 in 2003 as a high point in his career. 'It was basically just a big 767 with more engines and more people but with great destinations thrown in!'

***

As aircraft types have come and gone, the culture surrounding them has also evolved. Greg Miller describes the flight deck of those days flying the 747-400 as something of a mix, with very senior captains who had already been on the -400 for some time, younger pilots off the 767, and former Boeing 747-300 Classic captains all passing through the cockpit.

As with any closely shared working environment, sitting in a cockpit for many hours can range from a pleasant personal experience to a perpetual state of anxiety to see the end of it. Much of this depends on the personality of the captain, with the record showing that Qantas is no exception when it comes to differing personalities. Many former first or second officers on the 747 will tell you of a life of contrasts. There were captains who operated a very relaxed flight deck, always ready to pass on practical advice, thus providing a valuable learning environment.

'At the other end of the scale, however, were those whose idea of professional development involved yelling at you for the entire time you were flying and providing plenty of opportunity to demonstrate your lack of knowledge,' says Miller. 'Though they were small in number they were well known by all crew in the fleet, including the fleet managers, but often there was little done about it so they continued practising their "craft" unabated.'

Along with such 'personal anomalies', Miller credits the 747-400 as bringing a change in after-work culture. 'On one hand it was the party fleet. As a junior first officer you would be doing London and Frankfurt trips, with the odd five-day trip to Johannesburg thrown in for good measure and enough time even to take in visits to game parks or sporting events,' he remembers. As for the Kangaroo Route: 'We used to call the first night in Singapore southbound as "first night madness" and it was not uncommon to see the sun coming up on that one!' But such stopovers as Singapore involving multiple crews could also bring considerable educational benefits, providing crew members with the opportunity to compare notes and expand their knowledge.

Gradually, however, with the employment of what Miller refers to as 'the Gen Y pilots and crews', the social culture began a subtle move away from what had been normal for many years. 'Although the drinking culture was still alive and well, some of the younger crew now simply didn't want to participate,' Miller recalls. Eventually, along with the generational shift came a tightening of the airline's schedules, bringing shorter 'slip' times at en-route ports.

Now, with the 747 years behind them, times have changed for those like de Crespigny and Miller. While Miller is now a captain on the Boeing 787, de Crespigny, often the public 'face' of Qantas following the QF32 Singapore incident, has hung up his wings after a stellar career, one that began with him flying Caribou transport in the RAAF and concluded with the ultimate in airline jet captaincy.

13
THEY CAME IN
ALL SHAPES

While the 747-200s, a few -300s and eventually many -400s would comprise the bulk of the Qantas fleet, two very different versions of the 747 would bring their own unique imprint. The first of these was the 747 known as the Combi, designed to carry both passengers and freight on the same deck.

The Combi arrived in late 1977 after a long-running internal debate in Qantas about the 'questionable value' of freight when it came to sacrificing passenger seats for cargo pallets. Mixing passengers and cargo had often been the subject of banter or light-hearted exchanges when the various arms of the company gathered at the numerous conferences or in-house meetings. Not even the speed advantages brought by the jet age had done much to help the Qantas cargo cause at such gatherings, despite the fact that even before the 747, airlines like Pan American had used dedicated 707 freighters to cash in on the booming demand for carriage of large computer modules and other bulk freight items from the US. Even when management agreed to convert several of the 707-338s to carry a mix of 96 passengers and four pallets of freight on the main deck, the freight people remained unsatisfied.

So, while the rest of the company delighted in the arrival of the larger, wide-bodied 747, those in the cargo division believed their value had once again been overlooked. Anyone with the misfortune to have the word 'cargo' or 'freight' in their position description, they believed, were among the airline's forgotten people. And, rubbing salt into the wound, they now faced the innovation of a catering galley in the cargo hold of the 747, robbing them of even more space. 'If this was such a valuable innovation then why did only two other world airlines follow suit?' was former freight executive Max Hill's acid comment.

It would take four years after the arrival of the first 747, and the establishment of a cargo task force in 1975—its official role to 'formalise the company's position on air freight'—for change to occur.

Even then, despite considerable evidence of freight backlogs, the airline's cargo staff faced a daunting task, with research revealing the freight market's massive directional imbalance. Eighty per cent of freight was inbound to Australia, and a mere 20 per cent was outbound. Confronted with such 'unhelpful' statistics, they realised they had to abandon any desire for a dedicated 747 freighter.

Thus the compromise came with the Combi. Capable of carrying 270 passengers, it also allowed for 29 tonnes of cargo pallets on the rear section of the upper deck. The first of three Combis would be ready for delivery in late 1977, and it would need cargo terminals to handle it.

Unlike the lavish international passenger terminals dripping with all the modern customer-service conveniences, cargo terminals in the early 747 days were home to an assortment of oddly shaped containers, trolleys and tugs littering their interior and occasionally left out in the weather. Even long after the first 747s arrived in 1971, cargo was still being handled in a terminal on the Mascot Jet Base, where the Qantas cargo people and the cargo agency staff occupied sparsely furnished office space that was regularly repositioned to make room for more containers.

As demand increased, equipment breakdowns became common, particularly with what was known as the 'tram track', an electric device stretching over 90 metres or so, which was used to move the filled containers onto trolleys to be taken across to the international terminal for loading onto aircraft. Unfortunately, any breakdown meant the containers, ranging in weight from 1600 to 6800 kilograms, had to be moved into position manually. Little wonder, then, that former New Zealand manager and now cargo manager Norm Leek often heard his storemen refer to those 90 metres as 'Valium Alley'.

Even when the US-based company Transact eventually commenced construction of a new cargo terminal alongside the international terminal on the western side of Mascot airport, Qantas head office continued to move people in and out of the planning for the project—the freight division still hadn't become much of a priority when it came to staff continuity. According to Leek, there was no benefit from being too close to the airline's head officer when planning decisions for the new terminal were required, either. Inevitably, the first question asked by Transact's design chief Herman Wolfenbuttel whenever he visited the site was, 'Well, Norm, who's in charge this month?'

Leek would later enviously watch the much smoother development of a similar new Qantas cargo terminal at Perth airport: 'They were helped by being a few thousand miles away from head office!'

Even after the arrival of the first Combi, the cargo people continued to push hard for company acceptance of the significance of their role, with Jim Bradfield, the director of cargo at the time, often inventing his own humorous comparisons when presenting at corporate marketing meetings. After first pointing out to his audience that once again most of the agenda items centred around passenger carriage, he'd open his presentation with: 'Air freight doesn't have an ego, has no different classes of travel to choose from, doesn't need in-flight catering or entertainment and doesn't earn frequent flyer points. And without freight there wouldn't be a profit.' He'd then throw up a chart that demonstrated that revenue achieved from freight was always very close to the total amount of profit announced in the company's annual report.

But even coming to conferences armed with such statistics, Bradfield often found he had to resort to imaginative innovation. The challenge was to retain the attention of his audience, particularly when his cargo presentation was first on the agenda the morning after a company dinner that had rolled on well into the early hours.

On one occasion in Manila, he resorted to opening his session with an aerobics workout conducted by an attractive female instructor. 'That certainly got their attention and I was even able to detect some recognition among the audience of freight's contribution to the company's bottom line,' he remembers.

But in at least one respect, Qantas's freight component would become a trailblazer. In the 1980s it became the first to employ code sharing, where airlines allocate a certain number of seats on their own services to a partner airline, particularly on thinly trafficked routes. It was a concept that would later be widely adopted in passenger carriage, but Bradfield says it was an arrangement particularly suited to air freight: 'It worked well in air freight as it didn't require any passenger demands such as in-flight service, so any competition between carriers was largely focused on price and the ground services provided.'

Thus the arrival of three Combi aircraft between 1977 and 1980 helped to satisfy the concerns of the airline's freight people, and they entered the airline without too much fuss. The same could hardly be said for the other 'different' 747 to wear the Qantas colours—the 747 SP.

14
AND THEY CAME IN ALL SIZES

While Qantas's Combi might have slid relatively quietly into the fleet in 1977, the arrival of the smaller, high-performance version of the Boeing known as the SP (Special Performance) four years later was marked by two contrasting receptions. The first was an initial avalanche of publicity as it demonstrated its prowess on a flag-waving joyflight along Australia's east coast and across the Tasman to New Zealand. The second was industrial action, resulting in a strike that would strand hundreds of passengers around the world and almost force Qantas to its knees.

Right from the earliest days of the SP's consideration by the company, its path to become part of the fleet was anything but normal. Late in 1973, the company's technical development department had begun looking at wide-bodied aircraft that might be used on the restricted runways at certain airports on its medium-range routes, where the use of the larger 747Bs was limited. Early contenders included the three-engined DC-10 and the Lockheed 1011 TriStar, until the possibilities of the Boeing 747 SP came into the frame. One of its obvious advantages was its commonality with the 747 fleet.

Designed to fly higher and faster, the SP was 14 metres shorter than the standard 747, yet its larger vertical and horizontal tail and a comparable amount of engine thrust gave it a 'sports car'–type performance when compared to its bigger counterpart. Boeing only built a handful of them, the first making its mark with Pan American between New York and Tehran and later across the Pacific. While the latter application would ultimately figure in the operating schedule, Qantas's initial plans for it were, at least in retrospect, somewhat bizarre—on the short hop across 'the Ditch' to Wellington, where airport limitations provided Qantas with a major advantage over competitive neighbour Air New Zealand.

Wellington presented unique problems for the big jets. In Qantas's case, a decade had passed since the last of their propeller-driven Electras had serviced the New Zealand capital, a situation that eventually forced the airline into the embarrassment of chartering seats and cargo space on Air New Zealand's DC-8s, jets that themselves were facing retirement. Along with Wellington's notorious weather patterns bringing vicious crosswinds, another problem was its runway, which, at around 1935 metres, was far too short to allow an aircraft even the size of Air New Zealand's new DC-10s to operate a commercially viable service.

Despite repeated attempts over the years by the airport's management and local authorities to extend the runway, using extensive land reclamation into Lyall Bay, efforts had proved unsuccessful. Now, with the coming of the SP, not only might such runway works be unnecessary but the aircraft might provide Qantas with an opportunity to plunder one of Air New Zealand's primary connections between its third-largest population centre and Australia's east coast.

But even when director of flight operations Alan Terrell suggested the idea of an SP for Wellington to chief executive Keith Hamilton, he met resistance. Hamilton, it turned out, had already done some homework of his own. 'Boeing tells me it won't work,' he told Terrell. Convinced it would, Terrell set off to Seattle in an attempt to prove otherwise, taking with him the calculations of his small team of pilots and performance engineers. Soon he was back, returning with Boeing's own revised calculations, to finally convince Hamilton it was possible.

Next, Terrell's team set out to convince a sceptical New Zealand civil aviation authority of the safety aspects by developing the SP's own specific operating requirements for Wellington. Part of this involved painting special touchdown markings for pilots to aim for on the short runway as they approached to land. If there was any chance a pilot might miss touching down on the markers, there would be a mandatory go-around for another attempt.

But by then the question of how many SPs Qantas required for the service had raised another issue. Any plan Qantas may have had to only order one SP were complicated by the New Zealand government insisting there should be two, ensuring continued operations in the case of unserviceability or during maintenance requirements.

With plans now advancing rapidly towards a start-up, Qantas began work on a targeted advertising campaign on New Zealand television, highlighting how this new aircraft would bring Wellington into the jumbo era. So, among the usual batch of engineers and pilots heading for Seattle to prepare for the SP coming into service, was the airline's advertising manager Bruce Tregenza, who would work with Boeing on filming the necessary air-to-air footage of this new entry into the Qantas fleet. For Tregenza, the exercise would turn out to be much more fraught than a normal filming assignment.

Although air-to-air filming has been around since the days of wood, wire and fabric aeroplanes, it's probably fair to say flying a large aircraft like the 747 in close proximity to another jet is not something the average conservative Qantas pilot enjoys. That became abundantly clear to Tregenza at the pre-flight production briefing between two Boeing-based Qantas captains, Laurie Clark and Alan Bones, and the crew of the Learjet to be used for the filming. In keeping with Qantas's emphasis on matters of safety, Clark and Bones expressed some nervousness over the operational requirements for the exercise.

Tregenza could see their point. The Lear aircraft hired by Boeing was operated by Clay Lacy Aviation and would be flown by its owner Clay Lacy, himself a DC-8 captain with United Airlines. Lacey's Lear came specially equipped with two 35-millimetre Panavision cameras, each attached to one of two periscopes protruding through the top and bottom of the Lear's hull, ideal for filming as the Lear circled above and under the Boeing. 'The nature of the fittings meant that each camera operated with a fixed lens, so all changes of focus, such as zooms, had to be [made] using the Lear itself, which would mean that the SP and the Lear would at times be flying at extremely close quarters,' Tregenza recalls.

Tregenza noted that Lacy, with long experience in this work for Boeing, was 'calming in his encouragement', taking pains to assure Laurie Clark that all he had to do was maintain an even speed and direction with the SP. They would both keep direct contact over a 'open' mike so that each would be able to advise of any flight changes. Despite such assurances, Tregenza couldn't help noticing that both Clark and Bones showed signs they would be relieved when it was all over. It soon became obvious that they were right to be nervous.

'So we took to the air,' Tregenza recalls. 'At some points the aircraft were flying in such close proximity that I swear I could see Alan Bones' five o'clock shadow through the window of the Learjet!'

For Tregenza himself, however, the worst was yet to come.

Specifically equipped for its filming task, the Lear only had seats in its cabin for the film director and the camera operator, both with headsets that enabled them to communicate with the cockpit. Tregenza, on the other hand, had no headset nor, for that matter, a seatbelt, forced to sit unrestrained on a metal camera box facing the rear of the Lear.

None of this presented a problem during the filming sequence, even while the Lear circled above and around the Boeing itself. Once filming was completed, the Lear trailed the 747 as the two aircraft crossed Puget Sound on their return to Seattle, and the crews of both aircraft exchanged thanks and congratulations over the radio. It was all very happy until Lacy suddenly accelerated the Lear, flew over the top of the SP, dived down in front of it and did a barrel roll, exclaiming over his radio: 'That was Clay Lacy signing off.'

Tregenza, sitting unrestrained on the camera box and with no communication with the cockpit, had no idea what was about to happen. 'Although the centrifugal force kept my delicate posterior on the camera box, the two guys facing me at the rear of the aircraft later reported that the expression on my face had to be seen to be believed.'

Tregenza remains delighted that, despite his unexpected tangle with gravity, the experience resulted in some excellent television commercials produced by Qantas's advertising agency Monahan Dayman Adams, part of a short, intense launch campaign for the SP in Australia and New Zealand.

To many, the campaign itself had a festival-like atmosphere as thousands of Wellington's citizens gathered around the airport early in March 1981 when, with Terrell in command, the SP arrived at Wellington to re-establish a regular Qantas link. Neither was the assembled crowd disappointed as they watched the SP come to a stop only halfway down the runway.

'We did put on a little bit of a show, although I must admit we really stood on the brakes as we wanted to demonstrate the capability of the landing,' Terrell confessed.

Less impressed, however, was Wellington's mayor, who greeted Terrell when he walked into the terminal. 'You bugger!' he said to Terrell. 'I've been trying to get an extra hundred feet on that runway for years. Now I'll never get it!'

***

Those at Wellington that day wouldn't be the last to be impressed by the SP's capability. Another would be one of the world's legendary aviators, US Air Force general Chuck Yeager. A decorated World War II fighter pilot, Yeager went on to a career as a test pilot, in 1947 becoming the first to break the sound barrier, reaching 660 miles per hour (1062 kilometres per hour) in a Bell X-1 rocket-powered aircraft. Such career exploits were a highlight of Tom Wolfe's bestselling 1973 book *The Right Stuff*, and the subsequent movie of the same name.

In early 1985, visiting Australia and New Zealand on his way home to the US after a tour of Asia, Yeager was invited by Alan Terrell to sit up the front with him on a Wellington operation. Terrell cancelled at the last moment due to other commitments, so it fell to another of Qantas's senior captains, Cliff Viertel, to invite Yeager into the cockpit as they prepared to descend into Wellington. Viertel knew Yeager was no stranger to the SP, having assisted Boeing in its early post-production days with its high-altitude certification trials at

La Paz, Bolivia. Wellington's sea-level runway, however, at half the distance of La Paz's 4000 metres, would present a striking contrast for the American.

'The arrival was flown under Wellington's usually challenging weather conditions,' Viertel dryly recalls. 'Chuck became very quiet at about 1500 feet on approach, saying something like: "You're not going to land on that, are you?" The touchdown was right on the target and we had the SP taxiing well before the end of the runway.'

Yeager patted Viertel on the shoulder as he left the cockpit, and later phoned Terrell to thank him: 'I would never have believed it!'

***

Before its debut into Wellington, the 'Pocket Rocket' or 'Stubby Puppy'—as the SP became known—had already proved to be a publicity magnet for Qantas. Even its first flight out of Mascot raised eyebrows when the pilot executed a spectacularly steep climb out, after using only a little more runway than the Cessna light aircraft that had taken off just before it.

To allow Qantas station staff the opportunity to test ground-handling procedures, Terrell and a small Qantas team then took the SP on a three-day promotional tour, first to Brisbane and the Gold Coast, then on to Townsville and Cairns. In between a series of courtesy flights and low sweeps over the coast, more than 25,000 people inspected the aircraft at the four Queensland ports, with queues at times extending hundreds of metres.

Inevitably, as with such occasions, there were the unpredictable moments. The SP was the first 747 aircraft with such a large wingspan to use Coolangatta's Gold Coast/Tweed airport, and the take-off thrust from its outboard engines played havoc with the runway lights, forcing the civil aviation department to replace most of them.

At the Breakfast Creek Hotel after that day's Brisbane courtesy flight, the team's airport services and standards manager Brian Chapman mingled briefly with a group of the hotel's local customers over a few drinks, only to see fifteen of them turn up at the airport next morning to announce he'd invited them on the SP flight. 'Fortunately for me we had plenty of extra seats,' Chapman confessed.

Once the promotional activity along the Australian east coast and Wellington was completed, preparations began for the SP to fill its two primary roles: the resumption of the Wellington service, and the introduction of the first Qantas non-stop services across the Pacific. In the meantime, however, dark industrial clouds had been gathering. Soon, a dispute over cabin crew staffing levels would turn into a bitter confrontation between the airline and Australia's union movement.

***

For an example of how differing staffing functions can complicate an industrial dispute, we need look no further than the strike that coincided with the introduction of the SP. The dispute centred around the size of the SP and the number of cabin crew needed to man it. Because the SP had around

100 fewer seats than the larger 747, the company's plan was to reduce cabin crew numbers from fifteen to twelve.

But as the introduction of the SP approached, it became apparent negotiations between the airline and members of its cabin crew had reached a stalemate. The Australian Council of Trade Unions (ACTU), which represented more than 5000 Qantas employees in Australia, began to show an increasing interest in the argument over staffing levels. For the ACTU, however, the issue wasn't primarily the number of cabin crew staff the company had allocated for the SP itself, but the opportunity it offered to confront the airline over an even more important problem for the union movement: Qantas's long history of using staff labour to keep its aircraft flying during strike action. For years, the ACTU had watched with frustration and anger as the airline rostered its management and executive staff on to carry out a range of functions at airports—from catering and loading baggage to cleaning aircraft—when union staff went on strike.

The dispute would also reveal another significant factor: the split allegiances among the cabin crew themselves. Qantas female flight attendants, as they were called at the time, were not members of the cabin crew union, but had their own organisation with closer links to the pilots' union than to the ACTU.

The crunch came on 5 February 1981, when stewards refused to staff the first scheduled SP service from Brisbane to Wellington. Their places were immediately taken by twelve flight attendants who didn't consider themselves part of the dispute. With that, the ACTU intervened and in a little more than a week the dispute had spread to the entire Qantas fleet, with much of the ACTU's ire directed at the airline's pilots and flight engineers, whom they claimed had carried out additional duties on board.

When attempts by Qantas to have the bans lifted failed, it soon became obvious that this was no simple industrial relations dispute. The cabin crew staffing issue became secondary as the bans spread across ACTU membership to aircraft refuellers and other critical service workers with ACTU membership. Qantas responded by immediately standing down any employee who refused to do their assigned task, and a mass walkout of 5000 Australian-based ground staff from seventeen unions followed.

It was against this background that the company, in its time-honoured fashion, would once again revert to the use of staff labour, not merely in areas such as airport handling or catering but even by training executive and administrative staff to act as cabin crew. To cover safety requirements, the usually deskbound staff would gather at the Qantas Mascot Jet Base after their day's work to undergo basic safety training.

'It was primarily how to do the safety briefing and the life jacket drill, but I must admit we didn't worry too much about the way they served the meals on board, which had already been trimmed down,' says former cabin crew services director Jim Bradfield. 'When their training was over we gave them a cap and a badge which said "I am your cabin crew".'

They would then take the place of Qantas's Australian-based staff, who would be immediately stood down when they refused to operate a flight. And to keep flying internation-ally and avoid ACTU-directed fuel bans, aircraft would be refuelled at the nearest overseas ports, both on inbound and outbound services.

Even then, offshore operations would have their bizarre side. Rather than face being stood down the moment their flight returned to Australia, several hundred cabin crew who had been working on flights overseas when the strike began continued to staff flights between overseas ports. Ironically, had it not been for them the airline would have been forced to cease operations.

Soon, however, the use of company staff created an unfortunate set of circumstances that would become part of the company's chequered industrial history. With spitting incidents and the odd scuffle between staff on separate sides of the dispute, and allegations of cabin crew 'tampering' with food on board—the latter threat quickly leading to pilots insisting on specially prepared meals—it didn't take long for the strike to reach a crisis point. At one stage, more than 100,000 passengers were affected across the airline's worldwide network and no fuel was available for Qantas throughout Australia. Handling bans on aircraft also saw both the Australian and New Zealand governments step in to employ RAAF and RNZAF Hercules transports to airlift passengers across the Tasman. Such abnormal refuelling requirements would soon see Qantas Boeings flying over sectors that were not normally part of their route patterns.

In addition to the volunteers, some flights operated with all-female flight attendant crews, a situation that resulted in long-running bitterness between the two cabin crew groups. At least one flight operated without any cabin crew at all, with the emergency-procedures role handled by technical air crew on duty in the passenger cabin.

By early March, with the Industrial Relations Tribunal and the Commonwealth Conciliation and Arbitration Commission still struggling to bring the parties together, the first signs of a settlement began to appear when chief executive Keith Hamilton made direct contact with the ACTU's president Cliff Dolan. By mid-March, it was all over.

For Qantas, it had been a costly experience. While it had managed to keep operating, it had lost millions of dollars in revenue and additional flying, and thousands of its passengers had been affected, some of them stranded around the world. Many of those in Qantas would later conclude that the strike had resulted in no real winners. Although the final agreement saw the end of the use of staff labour by the company during strikes, distrust between the company and some of its staff would linger for years.

***

As for the SP, the aircraft originally at the centre of the dispute, it would continue to occupy a unique place in Qantas service—as a forerunner of the airline's daily non-stop services across the Pacific and, in the case of Taiwan, in achieving a significant milestone in international diplomacy.

The initial push for Qantas to introduce services to Taipei had its origins in Western Australia in the 1980s, when premier Charles Court, as chairman of the Australia–Taiwan Business Council, began pressing for an opportunity to encourage trade between his state and Taiwan. While studies had shown that Taiwan offered strong trade potential, partly with the export of seafood, mainland China's historical view of it as a breakaway province meant that any attempt by an Australian government–owned enterprise like Qantas to operate there would provoke a strong response from the Chinese government. Such a response could be expected to affect Qantas services to the Chinese mainland.

Surprisingly, however, Qantas soon learned that the Australian government supported the establishment of the link. Once again, it would be Alan Terrell who played a leading role in another SP initiative. When negotiations began, however, Terrell quickly learned that dealing with the unusual negotiating techniques of Taiwanese business leaders and government officials wasn't going to be easy.

'You'd spend the whole day thinking we had successfully negotiated some aspect and although they didn't encourage us to write anything down we would always go off and do so, only to have them say the next day they hadn't agreed to that!' Terrell remembers. Finally, after what he describes as 'a series of days of one step forward and two back', an agreement was reached, and the Qantas team prepared for the next step: walking a diplomatic tightrope with the Chinese government itself, to avoid putting at risk the airline's already well-established links with mainland China.

But if Terrell thought he would also be part of the team to

head for the Chinese mainland, he was soon to learn other-wise. That role would be taken over by a former public servant, one with extensive contacts in China—Sir Geoffrey Yeend. Letting Terrell down gently, Yeend explained that unlike most traditional government-to-government air service negotiations, in the case of China Qantas would stay in the background, leaving most of the dealings to Yeend and the Department of Foreign Affairs.

For Terrell, it would be a lesson in how delicate and even bizarre government relations could sometimes be. 'On one occasion, Foreign Affairs called to say they had written to the Chinese to explain what we were doing and the Chinese had responded by telling us what dreadful people we were and we couldn't do anything like that,' Terrell recalls. 'Foreign Affairs responded with an apologetic letter basically admitting what we had done. Then the two letters were exchanged and that was that!'

Other diplomatic nuances would mark the launch of services to Taiwan in 1990. One was the decision to strip the two SPs of their Qantas logos and livery and have them repainted in the colours of a new entity to be called Australia Asia Airlines. And not only would the airline's traditional 'flying kangaroo' on the aircrafts' tail be replaced by a 'dynamic ribbon' artwork, but crews operating the SPs would have their Qantas uniforms replaced with new ones specially designed for the service. Such examples of 'Chinese walls' lasted for six years until Qantas's privatisation in 1993, after which the airline could service Taiwan in its own right.

Boeing 767s replaced the SPs until the Australia Asia Airlines services ceased to operate in 1996.

***

While the SP's long-range capability when compared to the standard 747 suggested its primary route would be the carriage of passengers non-stop across the Pacific, former Qantas freight executive Max Hill considers its value in cargo uplift was often overlooked, even by many within Qantas. Although its freight capacity was limited over the long Pacific sector, the SP's Sydney–Wellington service provided a dramatic increase in cargo uplift, particularly with pallets of fresh New Zealand seafood destined for Japan, which could be transferred within hours at Sydney onto QF21 services direct to Tokyo.

Hill remembers that, as with other Qantas 747s, the SP occasionally carried some unusual loads. 'I remember in its cargo hold on one memorable SP trip across the Tasman were six million doses of sheep vaccine, 1.3 tonnes of hair dryers and one dog—breed unknown.'

Seemingly true to its record, however, right up until its final days with the airline the SP still managed to raise a few eyebrows, even on the Qantas board. For some years it had been customary for carefully selected senior executives to be the guests at the board lunch at the conclusion of its monthly meeting. Any invitation to such affairs was usually preceded by a quiet warning from Keith Hamilton to ensure those offered the privilege were conscious of the implications of any wayward comments that might embarrass management.

When it became the turn of one of Hamilton's closest colleagues, director of engineering Doug Scott, to attend the lunch, perhaps his chief executive should have realised the risk involved. Although widely respected, Scott was renowned for occasionally delivering a descriptive phrase that landed him in a spot of bother. Once he had caused a minor industrial incident among staff at his Jet Base when he told a union official that if several of his members continued to threaten strike action he'd 'take to them with a chunk of four-by-two'.

It just so happened that at the meeting before Scott's attendance at lunch, the board had been advised that an African airline had shown interest in purchasing one of the company's SPs and, as the conversation rolled around the dining table, one of the female board members asked Scott if he was sure the SP could perform the task required of it by the African airline. 'I can assure you, my dear, it will go down the runway like a dog with worms!' Sadly, there's no record of the subsequent conversation which took place in Hamilton's office.

As for the two Qantas SPs: both would play a significant part in Qantas service until ferried to their 'retirement' at Pinal Airpark, Arizona, in the early 2000s, where they were ultimately broken up for scrap.

15
CHRISTENINGS—A TALE OF POLITICS AND MEDIA JUNKETS

Ever since the first rolled off the assembly line at Everett in July 1971, the Boeing 747s have been media magnets, offering an opportunity for both Boeing and Qantas to unearth a veritable goldmine of media exposure at minimal cost to the airline.

That first delivery flight of VH-EBA *City of Canberra*, under the command of veteran captain Roly Probert, carrying more than 100 VIP and media guests all catered for with first-class service, was a media extravaganza. It set a pattern that would continue, although in a much more refined form, for years to come.

At *City of Canberra*'s first stop, an overnight at Honolulu, those aboard were treated to a spectacular Luau before resuming next morning for the final leg to Sydney, by which time not one drop of the champagne or the four dozen bottles of wine loaded in the United States had made the distance.

Neither did any of the specially hand-etched Captain Cook tankards, designed for exclusive use in the upstairs lounge, having been souvenired by those on board.

Although the full extent of the glitz and glamour of that first Qantas 747 arrival would not be repeated, it nonetheless encouraged Qantas to expand on a valuable and cost-effective method of publicity. The result was the decision to offer invitations to dignitaries and the media to attend the 'christening' ceremony of each new aircraft in Seattle, before flying home on its delivery flight to Australia.

By comparison, the vast majority of the more than 1500 Boeing 747s made since the first flew in 1969 entered airline service with little ceremony beyond the handover of the purchase documents and a symbolic transfer of 'keys'. In Qantas's case, combining the handover with a christening ceremony that names each aircraft after a particular city or town has become a uniquely Australian custom, one that dates back to the introduction of the airline's first Boeing 707 in 1958.

But those at the airline charged with selecting the names of new aircraft were only too aware of the delicate balance necessary to achieve fairness and avoid unnecessary interstate arguments. Thus a strictly calibrated procedure was introduced to ensure that no state, no matter how large or small, missed out in the allocation process. The only exception to the rule was the priority given to Longreach and Winton, the two towns that marked the airline's birthplace in 1920.

With the arrival of the 747 era, this 'naming' idea morphed into a publicity masterstroke. The honour of a Boeing carrying your city or town to the world appealed to a broad political and media audience in Australia. Occasionally, of course, envy intervened.

Flight engineer Norm King recalls at least one occasion of parochial envy when the naming of a Qantas aircraft saw 'adjustments' being made even after it had entered service. One concerned the airline's nineteenth Boeing 747-238, named after the Western Australian city of Bunbury. Since many of the Tullamarine-based licensed aircraft maintenance engineers lived in the Melbourne suburb of Sunbury, one enterprising engineer used some cleverly cut pieces of aluminium high-speed tape to mask parts of the 'B' in Bunbury to make the letter 'S'. Thus *City of Sunbury* did several Melbourne-to-Los Angeles return trips before the amendment was discovered and its birth name reassigned.

As 747 deliveries continued, the ceremonies themselves became much less extravagant than that first one in 1971. Some in Boeing were known to quietly question the cost and relevance of it all, prompting one Qantas executive to suggest: 'We probably paid for it in the extra costs they charged us for the nose wheel!'

***

For the christenings themselves, the first invitations would go out to the federal MP for the city or town after which the aircraft would be named, and to the council mayor or shire president. Next came invitations to the local newspaper editor or radio station reporter. Then, a few days before the aircraft was due to leave the Everett factory, they would head off to Seattle in a first-class Qantas seat to experience several days' stay at Seattle's plush Washington Plaza Hotel, along with generous Boeing-hosted tours and dinners. Their chosen dignitary would crack a bottle of champagne on the nose of their aircraft before they all boarded it for its delivery flight to Australia.

Inevitably, once word got out, such all-expenses-paid sojourns became much sought-after. Still, not everything would go strictly to plan. Take, for instance, *City of Albury*, which—for at least one invitee—became a question of the right seat. The normal practice for Qantas when issuing the invitation to a first-class seat to the United States was to add the caveat that such seats would be available only on a 'seat availability basis'—airline parlance for seats not already occupied by paying first-class passengers. If a seat was not available, the invitee would be provided with a seat in business class.

While Albury's mayor, its newspaper editor and other invitees were quick to accept, the local radio station manager declined in a huff on the basis that if a first-class seat could not be guaranteed he was unwilling to accept, nominating one of his employees in his place. As it turned out, the delighted substitute was able to travel first class both ways.

As might be expected, other complications occasionally arose on these christening trips, particularly with such a potentially volatile mix of politicians and media living in such close proximity for almost a week.

The high point of the three days of generous Boeing hosting usually concluded with a farewell dinner at Seattle's

Space Needle, one of the city's most recognisable architectural features and a dining venue which offered a spectacular view of the entire city flanked by Puget Sound. Along with a farewell tribute to the visiting guests, such functions also provided an opportunity for the Boeing hosts and their partners to mix with the Qantas representatives on permanent posting to Seattle, and to relax in each other's company.

At times, however, things didn't go to plan, particularly on one occasion when the Australian Labor politician who would next day christen his city's aircraft used his 'Thank you' speech to deliver an ideological broadside at Boeing for manufacturing an array of bombers and missiles 'which are killing innocent people around the world'. Most of those attending didn't quite know where to look. The following morning, one of the senior Boeing executives was gracious enough to pass him the bottle of champagne to break against his 747's nose with a smile, acting as if nothing had happened. But such instances were rare.

There were also lighter moments for the Boeing hosts. During one visit, the mayor of the town after which the 747 would be named delivered a lengthy speech extolling his country town's premier attractions, even down to a description of its new shopping centre. Unfortunately, most of the audience's eyes were still on him when he sat down to enjoy his first mouthful of grain-fed steak, and were watching as he withdrew his fork—a chunk of steak and his false teeth came out with it. Eyes quickly turned away but there were doubtless some interesting conversations as the Boeing people drove home that evening.

Along with dining mishaps, the relaxed atmosphere and lavish hosting of the Seattle visits could bring other personal risks, as one Australian journalist found to his sorrow. After a Boeing dinner, followed by a further lengthy sojourn in the bar at the Washington Plaza Hotel, he made the mistake of phoning a lady friend back in Australia. After muttering several tender thoughts, he realised too late he had mistakenly dialled his home number and was talking to his wife.

***

As more 747s entered the Qantas fleet, the policy of hosting VIPs and media in Seattle for christening and delivery was gradually abandoned, and the general media focus also began to change. Media coverage shifted from reporting on airline industry progress, with all the attendant drama and excitement of the age of the big jets, to keeping watch on how the airline was responding to the demands of its government owners and the public. As with the transition of air crew at Qantas from those who had been in World War II service to those of the post-war era, there would be a similar changing of the media guard over the half-century of the 747 in the airline's service.

Many of the journalists who covered the arrival of the first 747s into Sydney in 1971 were characters in their own right, and had not only spent a lifetime reporting on the industry but occasionally had been participants in it. While the names of most of them would barely be recognisable today, even to anyone in the airline industry, journalists such as Norman Ellison and Jack Percival could claim to be part of the pioneering efforts of Australian aviation's progress all the way up to the 747 itself.

Born in 1896, seven years before the Wright Brothers plunged off that hill in Kitty Hawk, Norman Ellison became interested in aviation on his return to Sydney after serving in World War I. During his career at the *Daily Telegraph*, the *Daily Mirror* and the *Daily Guardian*, as well as writing articles for aviation journals and working for a time at the ABC, he was often referred to as 'Australia's leading aviation journalist'. Using his distinct advantage of personally knowing most of aviation's pioneers, Ellison also wrote several books, the most significant of which was *Flying Matilda*, which traced the historic achievements of Charles Kingsford Smith, Bert Hinkler, P.G. Taylor and Hudson Fysh.

Ellison's contemporary, *Sydney Morning Herald* aviation writer Jack Percival, had been part of the crew on Kingsford Smith's first commercial crossing of the Tasman from Gerroa, south of Sydney, to New Zealand in 1933. Like Ellison, he too experienced war, but from a very different aspect. Posted to the Philippines as the *Herald*'s war correspondent at the outbreak of World War II, Percival and his then-pregnant wife Joy were captured when Manila fell to the Japanese in early 1942. Fortunately both of them, along with their newborn son, survived the war. Repatriated back to Australia in 1945, Percival resumed his role as the *Herald*'s aviation correspondent, once again writing himself into history as a crew member of P.G. Taylor's first crossing of the South Pacific from Australia to South America in March 1951.

While Ellison and Percival recorded the early and post-war years of Australian aviation, another of their era, Stanley Brogden, would see it through the early jet era to the Boeing 747. Beginning as chief of RAAF public relations, Brogden was then appointed the first aviation correspondent of Rupert Murdoch's national newspaper *The Australian* in the 1960s. Later moving to *The Australian Financial Review*, he was often welcomed into the inner sanctums of the likes of Hudson Fysh, Reg Ansett and TAA's chief John Ryland as he recorded the politics of Australia's often controversial Two Airlines Policy and the negotiation of Australia's international air service agreements.

Although not widely known, he could also take credit for initiating a change in another aviation icon—the coloured roundel insignia carried on the fuselage of today's RAAF aircraft. While working with RAAF public relations during the Korean War in the early 1950s, Brogden drew attention to the fact that, alone among the UN forces, the RAAF's No. 77 Squadron fighters still had no identifiable national symbol beyond the traditional roundels of the Royal Air Force. At Brogden's suggestion, the kangaroo was painted into the insignia of the 77 Squadron jet fighters and it began to appear on an ad hoc basis until it was formally incorporated by the RAAF in 1956.

Bizarrely, despite achieving an international reputation as an aviation writer and writing numerous books on the subject, Brogden had an intense fear of flying. His associates were occasionally in awe of the often-imaginative reasons he could come up with for not accepting an airline's offer of a seat on an inaugural flight, or some other promotional activity that required him to board an aeroplane.

With a unique reliance on his memory and rarely taking notes during an interview, he could also often be self-effacing, perhaps best summed up by Brogden himself in 1993 and recorded by Melbourne *Age* aviation writer Gerry Carmen in a tribute to Brogden after his death in 2008:

> Nobody ever came into half a century of professional work with such a complete lack of qualifications as this writer ... he had never been in an aircraft, never wanted to be in one, and was closer to Luddite principles than the admiration of complicated machinery.

***

While the scores of aviation journalists who progressively succeeded Ellison, Percival and Brogden into the 747 era are too numerous to mention, they fulfilled a vital role: not only keeping the public abreast of an exciting and ever-changing industry but also ensuring a critical eye was kept on those responsible for its operational and political decisions. Their focus on Qantas would become much sharper, particularly as the airline transitioned from government ownership in a tightly controlled domestic and international sphere to privatisation and more 'open skies'.

And along with the surge in passenger numbers during the Boeing 747 era came the journalists on what was known as 'the Mascot beat'—those who spent their early mornings interviewing international VIPs and entertainment stars as they arrived in Sydney, occasionally causing their aviation counterparts to recoil in embarrassment at some of their questions. Ted Porter, the ABC's aviation correspondent at the time, recalls one of them asking a stunned celebrity: 'Well, what do you think of Australia?' resulting in a puzzled smile from the new arrival who hadn't yet passed through the terminal.

Media changed too, and with the arrival of social media came new challenges for the airlines and cruise lines in managing their public image. Even as late as the 1990s, any incidents that occurred aboard an aircraft or a cruise liner might have lost their news value by the time the flight or cruise reached its destination. With today's widespread internet access, however, social media like Facebook and Twitter are often the front line of news, breaking a story long before the traditional newspapers, radio or television stations. Such a situation can often place an airline like Qantas at a disadvantage when it comes to controlling the narrative of a media storyline.

Increasing traffic demands over the years would also require 'outside' 747s to be brought into the Qantas fleet at times, not all of them quite so attractive as a pristine new Boeing out of Seattle. Former Qantas captain Cliff Viertel can attest to that.

16
HI HO, HI HO, IT'S INTO THE AIR WE GO

It was early 1988 when Qantas, already short on aircraft capacity for its own operations, started to look around the world for an extra 747 to meet its ongoing commitment to provide an aircraft on lease to Fiji's national carrier Air Pacific.

Quick research worldwide soon found what might be the best option—a Boeing with the UK registration G-HIHO, which had been operated by the Scottish airline Highland Express and was currently parked in Brussels awaiting the resolution of some outstanding maintenance costs that its owners owed to Sabena, the Belgian airline. Although it was an early -100 series 747, its flight deck and interior layout were close enough to the rest of the -200 aircraft in the Qantas fleet to make it a worthwhile proposition. A plan was put in place to fly it to Singapore, where SingAir Maintenance Services would undertake a complete overhaul before its final delivery to Australia.

At first sight, however, the aircraft's relatively poor overall condition prompted Cliff Viertel's delivery team to seek urgent advice from Boeing in Seattle, who immediately advised them not to touch the aircraft until Qantas engineers had gone over it with a fine-tooth comb. After they confirmed it as airworthy, Viertel should skip any test flight but carry out a very thorough pre-flight check, and even then delay departure if bad weather or turbulence was forecast. Once the plane was airborne, they advised, Viertel should limit pressurisation cycles as much as possible.

By late February 1988, Qantas engineers had given the clearance Viertel needed. With his team ready to leave, Viertel made a request for enough fuel to start the engines and carry out a systems check on the aircraft. That appeared to cause an immediate flurry among Sabena's legal people, who wished the Boeing to remain security for their debts.

Viertel describes what followed as having all the makings of a farce. 'First, they instructed the Sabena staff to "take the ignition keys" so we couldn't sneak off to another airport. But as there were no ignition keys, their only alternative was to remove the start switch module from the cockpit.' And, just for added security, they towed an Airbus A310 across the exit to the parking area, leaving no space for the Boeing to taxi past.

Therefore, Viertel hardly felt sorry for them when that night a North Sea gale ripped along the English Channel and into Brussels airport, dislodging a set of steel steps on wheels, sending them at first directly towards his Boeing, then crashing into the Airbus's nose, causing substantial structural damage. 'When we arrived next morning we wondered why so many dark, unfriendly looks came our way as we walked through the hangar,' Viertel remembers.

Several days later, with the 'keys' problem overcome, the 747 was fully loaded with fuel and, with only the crew and the Qantas engineers on board, G-HIHO took to the air. The hope was to make Singapore direct, although, as Viertel would discover, 'taking to the air' was not quite an adequate description of the thirteen-hour flight that followed. Their route took them into a right turn over Germany, across the Alps and the Adriatic to Egypt, then west of Cairo to Colombo and Thailand, and to Singapore.

Even the take-off, with HIHO's early Pratt & Whitney JT9D-3A engines and a full fuel load, was not a pleasant one. Twice, Viertel called on his flight engineer John Richardson for maximum climb thrust when the Boeing seemed to stagger into the air, only to hear an annoyed voice come back: 'You've got it!'

It took some time to reach their cruising altitude and not before a sequence of air traffic control route adjustments and terse exchanges with military air traffic controllers over the Middle East, who queried this unscheduled 'intruder' entering their airspace. Viertel's second officer became increasingly concerned that the missile-warning device sitting on his chair might become 'active'. Then came a brief, lighter moment after a gruff voice asked for their final destination. To their surprise, when they confirmed it was Singapore and on to Sydney, the reply came back in a broad Australian accent: 'Bye mate—say hullo to Bondi!'

Although initial calculations predicted they would have just enough fuel to reach Singapore, once in the air they noticed their Boeing was using an excessive amount of it, leading Richardson to suspect it might be coming from air leaks in the pressurised hull. By selectively switching off the aircraft's series of air conditioning packs, he was able to trace the fault to the lower cargo deck. Slipping through a trapdoor in the cabin floor to investigate, he was met with a loud rush of air and a chunk of sky showing through the surrounds of the rear cargo door.

It wasn't just a case of a leaking seal. There wasn't a seal there at all.

Such was the condition of the aircraft that after arrival in Singapore it took Richardson 30 minutes to enter its string of defects into HIHO's log before handing it over to SingAir to bring up to a safe operating standard. It finally reached Sydney five weeks later, where it operated for another year under the new Australian registration of VH-EEI, thus subsequently referred to by both Qantas and Air Pacific crews as 'EIEIO'.

Viertel, however, was wrong if he thought his daunting experience of G-HIHO/VH-EEI was over. Several months later, when asked to help a senior Air Pacific captain test the aircraft's automatic landing on a flight into Nadi, Viertel was within seconds of touchdown when the control column suddenly snapped back, causing the undercarriage wheels to crash onto the runway with such force that oxygen masks dropped down from above the passengers.

As a result, as he took up his customary position outside the cockpit door to farewell the passengers, his Air Pacific colleague was treated to some quizzical looks as they filed past. One commented to Viertel: 'I would like to have you for dinner at my village. My grandfather has a large pot for the purpose!'

EEI continued to fly around the Pacific before returning to Britain in 1990 to be scrapped.

Joe Sutter, acknowledged as the 'Father of the 747'. *Boeing*

Qantas chief executive Bert Ritchie chairs a meeting of the airline's senior executives in the late 1960s, when the company was planning for the introduction of the 747 to the fleet. Long-time director of flight operations Captain Alan Wharton is second on Ritchie's left while engineering's Ron Yates, later to become the airline's chief executive, is at left foreground. *Qantas*

Qantas Seattle representatives Ken Gould (left) and Michael Ryan hold the banner shortly before the departure of Qantas's first 747-200, VH-EBA, from Seattle in 1971. *Boeing*

Ken Gould and Michael Ryan look on as Qantas technical director Bob Walker inspects the lower lobe galley on the airline's first 747. *Boeing*

The airline's two HS-125 trainers escort the 747 into the Sydney airport terminal for the first time in 1971. *Ron Cuskelly*

Former wartime pilot and popular Qantas chief executive Captain Bert Ritchie in the early 1970s. *Qantas*

Another of the airline's best known captains, Alan Terrell, 'flying' his desk.
Qantas

One of the most important safety innovations of the jumbo era was the inflatable slide/raft for use in the event of a crash on water. It was developed by Qantas operations safety superintendent Jack Grant, who was awarded the Cumberbatch Trophy by the Honourable Company of Air Pilots for his invention. *Qantas*

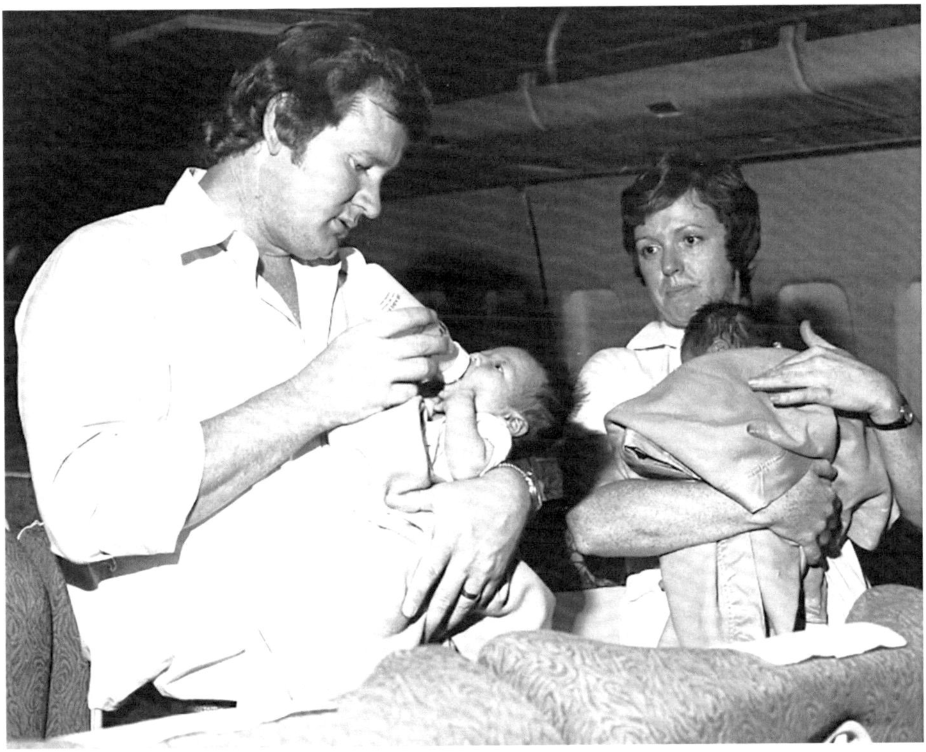

Flight steward Ray Finn takes care of one of the 194 orphans airlifted out of South Vietnam during Operation Babylift in April 1975. *Ray Finn*

Qantas manager Darwin Ian Burns-Woods and his wife Gabrielle inspect part of the damage from Cyclone Tracy in December 1974. *Qantas*

The famous seventies Qantas 747 Captain Cook Lounge; a feature of the airline's earliest 747s which would soon be converted to normal seating. *Qantas*

Qantas chairman Sir Lenox Hewitt in conversation in the Captain Cook Lounge.
Qantas

Boeing and Qantas officials at the christening ceremony for the 747 *City of Swan Hill* before its departure from Seattle in November 1979. *Qantas*

Hundreds lined up at the Gold Coast to inspect Qantas's first 747 Special Performance aircraft *City of Gold Coast/Tweed* on its promotional tour of Queensland in 1981, shortly before a cabin crew strike affected the airline's services worldwide. *Qantas*

New Zealand photographer Nick Servian captured the Qantas SP landing from a spectacular angle at Wellington in 1981. *Nick Servian*

Captain Ken Davenport's notorious 300-feet flypast to open the Oshkosh air show in the United States in the early 1980s. Unfortunately for him, it led to his demotion for six months when the Civil Aviation Authority insisted he only had permission to fly at 500 feet. *Unknown*

The author posing with VH-OJA *City of Canberra* at Boeing Seattle before it flew to London to begin a non-stop record between the UK and Australia in August 1989. *Jim Eames*

The flight crew of the record-breaking non-stop 747 delivery flight from London to Sydney in 1989. From left: captains Rob Greenop, David Massy-Greene, Ray Heiniger and George Lindeman. *Qantas*

City of Canberra makes it final landing at Albion Park after being donated to the HARS aviation museum in 2015. *Qantas*

The crew of the *Spirit of Anzac* on arrival at Istanbul for the Gallipoli Landings 75th anniversary in 1990. Captain Les Hayward, whose father served at Gallipoli, is at the bottom of the steps. *Qantas*

Digger Jack Ryan at Gallipoli in 1990 for the 75th Anniversary of the landings. When met at the foot of the aircraft steps in Istanbul by a Turkish veteran of the same campaign his comment was: 'It's great to be back—as a cobber!'
ABC/Vedat Acikalin

Qantas Captain Cliff Viertel, manager of 747 flight training, experienced some interesting 'airborne moments' during a long Qantas career. *Cliff Viertel*

Trevor Jensen's 747 at Mogadishu airport after lifting United Nations peacekeeping soldiers from Australia's 1st Battalion, Royal Australian Regiment, to Somalia. Flight Engineer Norm King remembers hearing the sound of gunfire as the aircraft prepared to depart. *Norm King*

Captain Trevor Jensen, in the pilot's seat, and tennis champion Evonne Goolagong-Cawley, during a flight to celebrate the airline's 75th Anniversary in 1995. *Trevor Jensen*

Not the best publicity for an airline: Boeing 747-400 VH-OJH overran the Bangkok airport runway in September 1999. *Australian Transport Safety Bureau*

An Australian Special Forces night-time training exercise on a Qantas Boeing 747. Such exercises were a regular occurrence in preparation for a hijacking incident. *Unknown*

A crowd gathers around *City of Canberra* at Albion Park in July 2020 to await the flypast of the last Qantas 747, *Wunala Dreaming*, to leave Australia. *Howard Mitchell*

Bomaderry photographer Howard Mitchell's spectacular air-to-air shot of *Wunala Dreaming* as it passes over the Wollongong area while departing Australia. *Howard Mitchell*

Captain Owen Weaver's imaginative flying roo signature was part of his flight plan to mark the departure of the last Qantas Boeing 747 in July 2020.
Owen Weaver

The landing of *Wunala Dreaming* in the Mojave desert as it arrives at its final destination as a Qantas plane. *Dylan Phelps*

17
INTO THE RECORD BOOKS— NON-STOP ACROSS THE WORLD

Australia's remoteness has always presented challenges to its national airline. Qantas is the oldest airline in the English-speaking world, and it has confronted difficulties of distance that few other airlines have had to face. To survive as an international carrier, it had to stretch the boundaries of long-range air travel to their absolute limits—and it did so long before the advent of the jet age.

The beginnings of Qantas's long-range travel story can be traced back to the early days of World War II. In 1941, the Australian government recognised that the airline was already experienced in flying-boat operations, so it delegated its crews to take delivery of the RAAF's first long-range Catalina flying boats. Initially employed in protecting Australia's sea lanes from marauding German raiders, these Catalinas would soon fulfil a critical role in the war with Japan.

On paper, the Catalina delivery task would have appeared fairly straightforward for pilots and navigators who had already accumulated extensive experience operating flying boats from Australia to Singapore and beyond. What made the assignment different, however, was the way captain Russell Tapp and his crew decided to use it as an opportunity to test their steed.

Technically, the requirement for the three-stop delivery flights was fairly simple: initially to fly 2680 kilometres from Pearl Harbor to Canton Island in Kiribati, to be followed by 3057 kilometres to Nouméa and then, finally, 1720 kilometres to Sydney's Rose Bay. But while that might have been the standard pattern for most of the deliveries, when his turn came Tapp couldn't resist the temptation. Trimming back the fuel consumption, he decided to push the range of his Catalina to its limit, overflying Nouméa and reaching Sydney in one hop, covering almost 4800 kilometres in 24 hours.

Such pioneering efforts in the careful management of fuel by Tapp and the other crews during the deliveries would pave the way for the airline's record-breaking and top-secret 'Double Sunrise Service' later in the war—at times over 30 hours in the air between Perth and Ceylon, much of it through enemy territory, to keep the vital link between Australia and the UK open.

Even with the coming of the 707 jet age, such excessive range requirements saw Qantas operate the longest route sectors of any airline in the world. After the first of its new Boeing 747-400s rolled off the assembly line, it wasn't long before the company's original long-range experience came to the fore.

***

The temptation for Qantas to achieve something like a non-stop flight from London to Sydney had been raised some years earlier by London-based marketing executive Tony Luker, although Luker's original idea was to use a delivery of one of the airline's long-range Special Performance 747s.

Doubtless the idea had been long forgotten by the time it came to the delivery of the first 747-400 in 1989, but it didn't take long for a small group of the airline's flight operations people to again start the concept rolling. Not only could it be a massive promotion but it would also steal the limelight from traditional rival British Airways who, rumour had it, were planning their own special -400 delivery flight into Heathrow. Such an opportunity was guaranteed to reactivate that historic competitiveness between the two carriers that was never far from the surface.

A cloak of secrecy descended as a small team of Qantas pilots and performance engineers gathered behind closed doors to flesh out the possibilities, only too aware of the risks involved in attempting to use a brand-new aircraft fresh off the assembly line. This would be not only a unique operational test but a scheme that ran the risk of becoming a public relations embarrassment if it failed.

The man that Qantas operations chief Alan Terrell appointed to lead the planning, captain David Massy-Greene, was a natural choice. Dux of the first Qantas cadet pilot scheme in 1965, he had flown Boeing 707s as a pilot and as a navigator before his promotion to captain on the 747 in 1984, and later filled the role of fleet captain on the Boeing 767 before his appointment as the project pilot for the yet-to-fly 747-400.

Given the complex array of organisational and operational issues that such a non-stop, long-range venture demanded, along with the need for secrecy, Massy-Greene's extended periods quietly gathering information as VH-OJA took shape in Seattle required him to exercise extreme caution. His colleague Alan Bones describes the atmosphere: 'As a member of a small team of executives, including British Airways, advising Boeing of each airline's particular requirements for the aircraft, he must have at times felt he was walking on eggshells. One slip of the tongue would mean the secret was out of the bag.'

Not that things were much different for yet another select group gathering at Mascot. Their critical function was to obtain the one element upon which the project would succeed or fail: aviation fuel.

First, they needed to fill the tanks with enough fuel for the flight itself, which they did using a very different method to the one used for a scheduled 747 passenger service. Bizarrely, the team's calculations showed that filling the tanks individually in the cool of the evening before departure until the fuel literally 'spilled out' of the wing vents would allow the fuel to contract overnight, thus providing space in the tanks for an extra 500 to 600 imperial gallons (2273 to 2728 litres) the next morning.

Second, they needed to determine the special type of fuel required, which would ultimately be the most important challenge as far as fuel was concerned. As the weeks went by, Peter Brooks, the man responsible for negotiating the airline's worldwide fuel requirements, found himself receiving some strange inquiries from the airline's then chief operating officer John Ward.

First it was: 'What's the density of fuel in London?'

Brooks's initial response obviously didn't satisfy Ward, so several other questions quickly followed, until finally Ward let him in on the secret: if a non-stop flight was to be achieved they would need a special high-density fuel—and Brooks's task was to find it.

The next day Brooks was on a flight to London with a mission to find a substitute for the standard Jet A-1 fuel used by the 747s, only to discover the nearest example of the type required was that used in cruise missiles. When he fired off a query to Seattle to test that idea, Boeing came back with the news that cruise-missile fuel was so heavy it would cause the -400's wings to fall off.

In the end it was Shell, the company that had helped Qantas survive in its very earliest days in the outback, that looked like it might come to Brooks's rescue. They believed their subsidiary in Germany could produce the relatively small amount of the special fuel mix capable of doing the job, although even then the logistics required were formidable. Brooks was told ten tankers would be required to carry the finished product across Europe to London, and even then the blended fuel would need to be constantly shunted backwards and forwards in its Hamburg rail cars to ensure it retained its mix until it was loaded onto the ferry to cross the English Channel.

While Brooks manipulated the fuel problem, others back at Mascot were looking at trying to solve what was morphing into another logistical nightmare. A one-off flight would demand its own air traffic control route across the more than 9000 nautical miles between London and Sydney, requiring optimum fuel-saving altitudes while at the same time avoiding air traffic delays. This meant negotiating complex and specific overflight rights with the numerous governments along the route, with the inevitable result of accepting compromises with routing and altitudes. But by mid-1989, with some of the critical negotiations now at decision point and with the August flight only weeks away, the secret could be kept no longer.

***

On 26 July, Qantas director of flight operations Ken Davenport announced the airline's plans to use the flight 'to validate the 747-400's performance data and fuel management techniques', while at the same time entering the aviation record books, surpassing a South African Airways 747 SP which held the non-stop record of 8872 nautical miles from Seattle to Cape Town. Davenport also announced the three operating captains who would accompany Massy-Greene: flight operations training director Ray Heiniger, flight standards and safety director Rob Greenop, and manager flight simulator George Lindeman.

Additional passengers on board would be limited to 23, and included board director Jack Davenport; representatives of Boeing, and engine and oil companies; and a small, carefully chosen group of journalists, several of whom would provide live radio feeds as *City of Canberra* crossed the world. To reduce weight, even their baggage would come on a separate Qantas service. Carrying so few passengers, however, had its advantages: the flight would need only one heavy galley for provisioning meals, minimal water tanks and only one of the standard three air-conditioning packs.

In early August, with the aircraft now in Qantas hands, test and endorsements flights for the crew began over Moses Lake near Seattle. It was here that the first serious problem arose. Mysteriously, after around four hours of training and with their instruments showing normal oil pressure, other indicators started to reveal an alarming reduction in the amount of oil being used in two of the aircraft's Rolls-Royce RB211 engines. Ray Heiniger would subsequently describe it as an 'oil hide', but its initial discovery certainly created enough concern to put the whole plan in jeopardy. He promptly sent a warning telex to Rolls-Royce in England that they might need to have two spare engines on stand-by.

To everyone's relief, the problem would finally prove to be a by-product of the intense training regime the crew had put the aircraft through at Moses Lake, where the 747 had been consistently engaged for hours in left-hand turns in the circuit area. This consistent left turning 'bias' had somehow affected the readings on the engines on the 'downside' during the turns.

On the morning of 11 August, *City of Canberra*— watched by a small contingent of media specifically flown to Seattle to witness the occasion—took off on its positioning flight to London. The media group's size was in a striking contrast to what lay ahead in the UK, where anticipation of the record attempt was already attracting extensive press interest. Once in London, Massy-Greene and his crew were required to divide their time between a hectic schedule of official dinners and media commitments, and journeys back and forth to Heathrow to oversee preparations for the flight.

There's little doubt it was a difficult four days for British Airways. Here, on their local turf, the former colonials were getting front-page coverage in London's *Daily Telegraph* and dominating night-time television, culminating in a congregation of media at Heathrow on the morning of 16 August as special arrangements were put in place to prepare VH-OJA for flight. Its take-off would bear little resemblance to a regular Qantas 747 departure from Heathrow's passenger terminal.

On this morning, *City of Canberra*'s engines would not be started immediately after push back. Instead, those on the tarmac watched the 747 in awe when, with its tanks so full, fuel began rolling off the wingtip vents as the aircraft was towed to the end of the runway. Since his calculations had shown the aircraft would use a half-tonne of fuel taxiing between the terminal and the start of the runway, Massy-Greene wanted to conserve every drop.

Then the engines were started, and it was in the air for a graduated climb through British airspace and across Europe. Air traffic controllers in a succession of countries had cleared the 'special' flight for the use of optimal altitudes to allow it to save on fuel, and on occasions would even move other aircraft out of the -400's way. When one airline pilot over Germany wanted to save fuel and requested the use of the same altitude as *City of Canberra*, he was quickly told by air traffic control they already had an aircraft at that altitude: 'And he's going a bit further than you are.'

First tracking over Germany and across Yugoslavia—where the Belgrade controller passed on the best wishes of the government—it flew over Turkey, Tehran and Muscat until heading towards Colombo. While the four captains took turns relieving each other in the cockpit and juggling flight levels as they watched fuel usage, Davenport and the few passengers on board kept themselves active by walking the empty aisles, and were served meals by two of Qantas's most senior flight service directors, Dave Cohen and Mal Callander.

But those on board were not to be totally denied a touch of Qantas's traditional first-class service. Due to weight restrictions, only 350 kilograms had been allowed for food and beverages, but the menu somehow managed to include Caspian caviar, oysters, poached salmon and, much to the delight of *Sydney Morning Herald* aviation writer Tom Ballantyne, two dozen cans of Foster's, a few bottles of champagne and a small selection of red and white wines. 'Someone obviously had been thinking of us,' an appreciative Ballantyne would later comment.

Over Colombo, as they climbed the aircraft to 41,000 feet to take advantage of more favourable winds, Massy-Greene and his crew might have allowed themselves a brief moment to recollect that directly below them were the waters where the wartime Qantas Catalinas from Perth had established their own long-distance reputation. It's doubtful any such thoughts lingered long, however, as those winds at 41,000 feet were destined to be the last in their favour. Once the aircraft was abeam the Cocosnds, Massy-Greene received the news he had been dreading: Sydney weather was expected to deteriorate, bringing with it intermittent thunderstorms around the time of their arrival.

From then on it would be touch and go as that traditional air crew dilemma presented itself: the necessity to handle diminishing fuel reserves yet still have enough to allow a diversion to an alternate airport. On this occasion, however, there was a world record at stake.

Meanwhile, monitoring their progress ahead of them in Sydney, Ken Davenport was busy working his open line to the weather bureau and, since an overly negative forecast might put the whole record attempt in jeopardy, gradually coming to the conclusion he might soon have to reach for his last resort: convince the bureau to alter the forecast from 'thunderstorms' to 'heavy showers', thus allowing Massy-Greene more margin with his minimum fuel requirement. To Davenport's relief, the weather bureau agreed and the revised forecast went over the radio to VH-OJA.

Unfortunately, a few moment later, with Davenport still on an open line to the bureau, a crash of thunder burst over the Mascot Jet Base:

'What the **** was that?' asked the bureau official.

After a few seconds of silence, Davenport assured him that no one at Mascot had heard anything.

Soon after, *City of Canberra* appeared out of the overcast skies to the north, sending up a cloud of spray as its wheels touched Mascot's runway and the record books—20 hours, 9 minutes and 5 seconds after lift-off from London. Hundreds of Qantas staff gathered to welcome the crew as they stepped from the aircraft. Standing in the rain, one Qantas engineer, when reminded of the British Airways plans to do a non-stop 747 flight from London to Perth, expressed his doubts as to whether it would attract much attention: 'I guess we've sort of stolen their thunder a bit.'

There were other comparisons of note that day: as a child in 1948, it had taken Massy-Greene and his parents a total of 93 hours, with six stops, to cover the same journey in a Lockheed Constellation. His compatriot George Lindeman could go one better than that: it had taken his great-grandfather nine months to reach Botany Bay in 1787–88.

***

At a Jet Base Open Day several weeks later, the Australian Youth Orchestra, The Seekers, Debbie Byrne and Normie Rowe provided the entertainment as Hazel Hawke, wife of prime minister Bob Hawke, officially christened *City of Canberra*. The aircraft's long-range record remained in place until June 1993 when an Airbus A-340-200 flew from Paris to Auckland in 21 hours and 32 minutes. Even that, however, still hadn't matched the 30-hour secret Qantas wartime flights between Perth and Colombo.

David Massy-Greene, the man primarily responsible for the success of the mission, would go on to deliver fourteen Boeing 747-400s into the Qantas stable, out of a total of more than 30. Its long-range capability would bring new opportunities for his airline, but for Massy-Greene it would be the prelude to a whole new phase of his career.

18
KEEPING 'EM FLYING

While he'll acknowledge the advantages the -400 brought to Qantas's long-range route structure, engineer David Forsyth still has the hint of a smile on his face when he describes the 747-400 as something of a 'hypochondriac'. The combination of its state-of-the-art 'glass cockpit' and its advanced technology wrapped within a computerised airborne environment, with all sorts of 'bells and whistles' going off in the cockpit, would at first prove a daunting prospect for both pilots and engineers.

As with most things in aviation, there's always an acronym to fall back on. In this case, it was the MEL, or Minimum Equipment List, a safety-based list of items required to be serviceable for the flight to proceed on the next sector. Long delays in -400 flights resulted, occasionally up to nine hours, as engineers on the ground at overseas ports conferred with those at Mascot to determine which items on the list of message alerts might represent a genuine fault, and which might be simply false alarms.

For people like Forsyth and his colleague David Cox, however, working with such issues even had its rewards. While Forsyth joined the airline's engineering department only months before the first 747 flew over Mascot's fence in 1971, David Cox arrived much later—in 1986—as part of the team chosen to evaluate the engines for the 747-400, which was then still under development as the successor to the 747-200 and -300.

If there is one common theme in both Forsyth's and Cox's recollections of their Qantas years, it's the deep respect and enduring connections that developed between Qantas, Boeing and the engine manufacturers—first Pratt & Whitney, then Rolls-Royce and General Electric. Cox suggests this in part went back to the 707 days and the years of pressure from Qantas for additional range and greater fuel efficiency, while at the same time keeping weight out of the aeroplane to achieve both. 'Often there would be airports with short fields or other restrictions and so there would be particular tricks required with the engine/airframe combination to make an aircraft viable, along with compliance with existing and future environmental legislation,' Cox explains. 'There was also the requirement to work with local rules, such as curfew requirements at places like London's Heathrow.'

Such issues formed the core of the conversations with Boeing: to get the required range, be able to fly out of all planned airports, optimise the interior for the type of operation planned, and get the environmental design right. So, for people like Forsyth, Cox and chief power plant engineer Scott Collins, the challenges presented by the engines on the 747, whether Pratt & Whitney, Rolls-Royce or General Electric, were part of a constant effort to push the 747's performance to its maximum.

Those early agonies over the Pratt & Whitney engines on Pan Am's 747-100 and the first -200s continued with the highly anticipated Rolls-Royce RB211 engine. According to Scott Collins, the RB211 suffered a significant performance shortfall when it came to the fuel-burn levels guaranteed by Rolls-Royce. Compressor-blade failures, and combustion and fuel nozzle problems also had to be overcome. As far as David Cox is concerned, however, such challenges had their upside when it came to the quality of the Qantas people he worked with.

The development and performance unit Cox joined to evaluate the engines for the coming -400 was led by Mick Cook, who would become something of a legend himself, commanding worldwide respect throughout the industry— including among the young engineers who worked for him. 'Cookie', as he was universally known, was born Laurence Ivan Cook but the nickname bestowed on him in his youth stuck with him for the rest of his life. Cox remains grateful for the opportunities that working under Cook provided.

'Being part of a small group, we got to see the Boeing– Qantas relationship at work,' Cox remembers. 'Teams would come down from all the manufacturers and engine makers to discuss their new products. We young engineers would then have the chance to undertake studies to test the capabilities of such products from an operational and economical point of view.'

Cox recalls one of the high points: the arrival of Joe Sutter himself to push the advantages of the 747-400. 'We all sat around the table and listened while the Qantas team debated with Joe how the aircraft could be improved. A number of changes to the design eventuated from that meeting, the most significant being an increase in the maximum take-off weight.' Mick was approaching retirement at the time and he wanted to ensure his expertise didn't leave with him, says Cox. 'He was very keen to pass on the legacy of technical information in the Qantas corporate memory, so he made sure we sat in such meetings and listened and learned from the debates.'

Cook also ran what became known as his 'Friday afternoon class', inviting in key people from other departments to explain their roles to Cox and his colleagues. 'For a young engineer straight out of university it was a fabulous start to a career!'

One of that group who was still working at the Qantas Jet Base the day the first 747 arrived in 1971 was engineering facilities manager Jack Avery, who had joined the airline as its first apprentice at Longreach base in 1927, where he trained under Qantas's founding engineer Arthur Baird. Later, during World War II, Avery supervised the overhaul of air force engines at Archerfield, until arriving at Mascot in 1945 as superintendent of the engineering and overhaul shop. Awarded the MBE in 1967 for services to aviation, he received his 45-year 'pin' five months before his retirement in December 1972. At the time he was the only person other than Hudson Fysh to receive such an award.

Not that Avery's long service was unique. Another of his colleagues, George Roberts, who retired shortly before Avery, had joined in 1936 and worked for the airline for the next 34 years. Those who followed credit them with keeping the Qantas ethos alive, and for applying their ingenuity to solutions that often saved the company a great deal of money as well.

One example came with a requirement in the early 747 to upgrade the original Pratt & Whitney -3A engines to the more efficient -7 version, a conversion exercise that involved the removal and reinstallation of hundreds of reshaped vanes. When the first estimate revealed the cost of sending the parts back to Pratt & Whitney in the US for reshaping would be in the order of $54,000, Qantas engineering sent out feelers to ascertain what it might cost to contract out the work locally in Australia. Even then, the best they could come up with was $20,000. The technical services department's Arthur Kelly believed he could do better than that and set about designing a rig himself—one capable of doing the job for $2000.

Engineering was not the only department with a reputation for saving on costs. The engineers' counterparts in flight operations were renowned for grasping every such opportunity, particularly when it came to the range advantages offered by the 747-400.

***

Former Qantas captain Murray Warfield likes to cite an unlikely comparison. Sydney's taxi industry, he says, had the edge over aviation when it came to one aspect of communication. 'Way back in the nineties, even they'd get all their messages on a screen,' he points out. 'It's called data link communication. Taxi company head office knew where they were because they had a GPS receiver and their transmission provided not only an accurate navigation aid but a surveillance system as well.'

When it came to aviation, however, even allowing for the impressive leap from the sextant to the sophistication of the inertial navigation system, any significant errors in such a system presented safety implications well beyond those of a ground-based taxi industry.

When you had aircraft moving at 24 nautical miles (44 kilometres) every three minutes through increasingly crowded air corridors, they needed to be kept at least fifteen minutes, or around 120 nautical miles (222 kilometres), apart. It was an expensive economic margin in a high-speed industry, but necessary to allow for such factors as drift errors due to winds and timing delays with normally efficient radio communications.

In some respects the development of the Future Air Navigation System—or FANS, as it became known—was the result of fortunate timing. In the 1980s, as new cockpit technology was being built into the Boeing 747, the International Civil Aviation Organization (ICAO), the United Nations body responsible for planning and developing aviation standards, had been studying what could be done to improve the efficiency and economics of aircraft separation requirements while at the same time ensuring acceptable safety margins.

Cut to Boeing's chief avionics engineer Dave Allen and his team, who accepted the challenge to build a software package for the -400's state-of-the-art flight management system. The package would use satellite and data links to refine communications, navigation and surveillance into an integrated system.

Warfield describes Allen's first attempt in the early 1990s, known as FANS–1, as 'having all the bells and whistles' but being far too expensive for airlines like Qantas to take seriously. That, explains Warfield, is where David Massy-Greene came in, calling for a much simpler, less expensive version of Allen's concept.

Although the European airlines showed little interest in buying it, those in Qantas, Cathay Pacific, Air New Zealand and United Airlines could see the advantages. And the wide-open spaces of the Pacific they operated in would be an ideal place to use it. Thus came the formation of a small informal group including Warfield working under the Massy-Greene–Dave Allen Boeing team, with the US Federal Aviation Administration, Honeywell, United Airlines and Air New Zealand, to eventually develop a FANS 'aviation package'. Its certification flying took place in Sydney in 1995, marking the first occasion any 747 Type Certification flying had been completed outside Seattle.

As a satellite-based system, FANS effectively eradicated any drift errors and radio-communication delays. It was capable of pinpointing precisely where an aircraft was anywhere in the world within the shadow of the aircraft itself, and it reduced aircraft separation requirements from around 100 to 30 nautical miles (185 to 55 kilometres). With the resultant radical changes to air traffic control systems on all major air routes, FANS saved millions by shortening routes and increasing airspace capacity, and by overcoming the necessity for some of the traditional ground-based navigation aids.

On the Pacific alone it reduced the flight time between the US and Australia by 25 minutes. Warfield, a trifle cynically, suggests that 'FANS helped move the aviation industry into the twenty-first century!'

While the advantages over the Pacific were obvious, the main challenge for Qantas was to use it to Europe. So Warfield developed a business case to convince the airline's board:

We knew we'd get our money back over the Pacific but to overcome the restrictions on the routes to Europe, which were costing us a lot of money, we needed to convince air traffic control agencies on that route of the advantages in purchasing and installing the FANS equipment as well.

I think the board had a problem grasping it all, with the result they dropped it back onto then managing director James Strong to make the decision to spend what amounted to $1 million per aircraft.

So he called in the airline's manager engineering Bob Schwartz and we walked around a few numbers until Strong said, 'Okay, we'll do it.' And with that he spent $24 million!

Massy-Greene and Warfield subsequently assisted the Chinese to use FANS to save 50 minutes on a new route from western China to Europe; the route also enabled them to avoid overflying occasionally volatile airspace in the Middle East and Afghanistan.

As for the Europeans' reluctance to accept FANS: by the late 1990s, with the package by now standard equipment on the new Boeing 777, the European pilots were ready to accept the concept. Warfield has his own theory about the delay with the European decision: 'I've always suspected when it originally came before European airline managements they might have had a problem with the fact that it wasn't invented there!'

***

Several international awards followed Massy-Greene's work on FANS, including the Guild of Air Pilots (now the Honourable Company of Air Pilots) Johnston Memorial Trophy and the International Air Transport Association's first Global Navcom Laurel award. Although there appears to have been little recognition of his work in Australia, on his retirement from Qantas in 1999, Boeing were quick to invite him to Seattle to be part of Dave Allen's avionics team, where he would continue to take part in another significant change in aircraft cockpits.

Anyone who has had a long association with aviation will recall the sight of airline pilots walking through airport terminals carrying their ubiquitous black leather flight bags, which contained the numerous manuals, aeronautical charts and other navigational paperwork necessary in an already cramped cockpit. Thanks to the work of Massy-Greene and Dave Allen, the bulky flight bag is today a rare sight, replaced by its electronic replacement—a specially designed iPad.

Murray Warfield retired from Qantas in 2014, and was the first former Qantas staff member to be appointed to the board of Australia's Civil Aviation Safety Authority.

19
KEEPING WATCH IN THE COCKPIT

You need only look back along the history of Qantas's fabled Kangaroo Route to London to see how the 747 changed the industry. Instead of a whole series of stops for refuelling and to pick up passengers, as in the days of the piston-engined Constellations, or even the reduced stops on the jets of the 707 era, the longer-range capabilities of the 747 eventually slashed the stopover points on the flagship QF1 Sydney-to-London route to just two: Singapore and Bahrain.

Of course there were variations, too—other flight numbers took in destinations such Bangkok and Kuala Lumpur in Asia, then Athens, Frankfurt, Paris, Amsterdam and Belgrade in Europe. As the years passed, so did the route structures. And much of the methodology involved in flying them changed as well.

Like many of his former colleagues, Roger Carmichael, one of Qantas's most senior captains from the airline's 747 era, paints a vivid picture of life in the cockpit along the Kangaroo Route in the years before technology began to make the pilot's life a little easier.

These were the days before the September 11 attacks in 2001, of course, when the odd passenger who was fortunate enough to be invited up to the cockpit probably went back to his seat with the impression that flying a Boeing 747 across the night sky might even be a trifle boring. In reality it was far from it.

'For instance, pilots needed to be "listening out" on their radio at all times in the event they had to avoid what might be an air traffic control error,' Carmichael explains. 'Therefore it was standard practice for the captain of the crew about to leave the cockpit at a stopover port to hand to the incoming crew a note showing all the other aircraft which would be operating in your vicinity, what altitude they were at and, in terms of minutes, where they were from you.'

The main reason for this was because, contrary to popular belief, the 'highway in the sky' has no firm lines in the middle of the road, as its earthbound equivalent does. Aeroplanes flying at almost 1000 kilometres per hour, even if travelling in the same direction, need to be separated by both distance and altitude. 'Listening out' ensured pilots were instantly alerted when they heard another aircraft's crew request a change of altitude.

'Violations happened all the time,' says Carmichael—to the point where, when flying along the narrow band of restricted airspace at night above the Middle East, Qantas crews would switch on their wing lights just to make sure aircraft coming at them knew they were there. 'I can remember once telling another aircraft to climb 500 feet while we would descend 500 until we passed each other, simply because air traffic control could not sort it out in time. In particularly dangerous areas across northern India and Iran, some airlines adopted the practice of always flying half a mile to the right of their track to avoid the possibility of a head-on at the same altitude.'

Such occurrences where crews could not rely on air traffic control were not uncommon. When one Qantas crew, again flying over the Middle East, heard air traffic control clear another Qantas 747 heading in the opposite direction up to their own altitude, the crew immediately switched on their landing lights and called their opposite number over the radio to alert them.

Such situations might not necessarily involve Qantas 747s. Crossing over the former Yugoslavia one morning, a Qantas crew heard Zagreb control clear a Boeing coming in the opposite direction to climb to a new flight level, clearly presenting an obvious risk to a jet the Qantas 747 pilots could see flying several thousand feet above them. When the Qantas captain alerted Zagreb to the imminent danger of a collision, the controller appeared to become confused and have difficulty understanding the problem.

'So we warned the aircraft coming towards us to keep a good lookout "as something might be coming through your window shortly",' Carmichael remembers. 'They immediately stopped climbing until they could visually sight the other aircraft.'

Air traffic control's range radar and radio position reports had, with some limitations, allowed it to track aircraft, but as time went on other aids, including the use of satellites, would be introduced to cater for aircraft flying over routes previously well beyond radar surveillance. Then, in 1989, came the introduction of the Traffic Collision Avoidance System (TCAS), which provided pilots with a remarkable improvement in situation awareness information. Along with its ability to provide crews with early detection of any aircraft in their vicinity, it offered a solution as well. However, the most experienced Qantas pilots would tell you that even a TCAS resolution would have been a last resort and there is no substitute for cockpit disciplines such as 'watching out' for other aircraft.

With rules prohibiting them from reading anything in the cockpit that is not operational, Qantas crews would probably wince at reports of the crews of some other airlines being distracted whiling away their time reading the latest stock exchange reports or browsing the internet through the aircraft's wi-fi, leading to the cynical comments by one 'old hand', 'What difference does it make what the pilot was looking at when the collision occurred?'

While technological advances have contributed to making the pilot's task easier, too much reliance being placed on them, along with a lack of basic flying experience among some pilots, is causing serious concern throughout the industry. Two of the more significant air crashes of recent times may have given weight to these concerns.

In June 2009, an Air France Airbus A330 flying from Rio de Janeiro to Paris crashed into the Atlantic, killing all

228 passengers and crew. Alarmingly, the subsequent investigation revealed the crew lacked the basic flying skills to understand the aircraft was about to stall.

Four years later, three passengers died and others were injured when, on a clear day, the crew of an Asiana Boeing 777 totally misread their aircraft's landing profile as they approached San Francisco airport, with the result they crashed into the sea wall short of the runway. Investigators later found that when faced with the airfield's instrument landing system being out of order, both pilots lacked the basic flying skills to execute a manually controlled landing.

In the 747 era, while Qantas reaped the benefits of its own disciplined training regime, it was also supported by a general aviation sector that provided an ideal training ground. Australia's open spaces and generally good flying conditions provided many future Qantas pilots with the opportunity to gain experience and hone their skills before entering the cockpit of an international airliner. The story of Qantas's 747 operations is not simply about pilots, however. There were others, like the flight engineers, for whom the advances in the 747 would mean a radical change in their role.

***

Beyond pilots, there have always been other specialists in the cockpits who have contributed to Qantas's record as one of the safest and most efficient airlines in the world. The airline's route structure and the long distances to be flown have always required crew numbers rarely matched by other international airlines, even as far back as Lockheed Constellations of the 1950s that carried a crew of seven—captain, first officer, second officer, two engineers, a navigator and a radio operator.

The arrival of the jet era with the 707 saw technical crew numbers drop to five, with the reduction of one engineer and the radio operator. With the introduction of the 747, the navigator also departed—leaving only the flight engineer and the pilots as the remaining links with the airline's earliest days.

Even then the word 'flight' had not always been part of their title—their original predecessors were simply called 'engineers', at times referred to colloquially as 'flying spanners'—taken along for the ride when some attention might need to be paid to the engines while the aircraft was on the ground. Qantas's historical records trace the ground engineer from its original DH-86 days, through the pre-war Empire, Hythe and Catalina flying boats and on to the post-war Lancastrians, DC-3s and DC-4s. But it wasn't until the L-749 Constellation in 1947 that a flight engineer was engaged as a permanent crew member on a Qantas aeroplane.

Back in the days of the Catalina, engineers did not have the most comfortable seat on the aircraft, wedged into a cramped space several metres behind the pilots in the pylon that joined the fuselage to the wing. With only a set of engine indicators and a row of switches, and receiving instructions from those in the cockpit via a visual signal system or over the intercom, the engineer's only outside view was from a tiny window slot at the side. Consider what that environment must have been like for engineers flying the secret Double Sunrise Service non-stop between Perth and Colombo during World War II, when some of the flights took up to 30 hours.

Former Qantas flight engineer Colin Lock joined the airline as an apprentice in airframes and engines in 1964, and served as a flight engineer for more than 30 years through the 707 and 747 eras. In his nostalgically titled *Finished with Engines*— a reference to the final call between the flight engineer and the aircraft's captain on shutting down the engines at the end of a flight—Lock has documented the story of Qantas's long-haul engineers, tracing their stories from the airline's beginnings to their final days with the introduction of the Boeing 747-400 in 1989. Along with providing an important window into a colourful period of the airline's history, it also highlights the often overlooked role played by the flight engineer, which tends to be overshadowed in the public's mind by that of the pilot.

Before the delivery of the airline's first 747B in 1971, a group of Qantas flight engineers was sent to Seattle, already equipped with up to twenty hours of classroom technical instruction, plus simulator and on-aircraft training. They found their new working environment was somewhat in keeping with the aircraft's size: the instrument panel had far more systems on display than they'd had on the 707, and the panel itself was more than twice as long. But now, at least, Boeing had assisted by installing an electrically driven seat that made it easier for the engineer to slide forward in the cockpit and to operate the thrust levers during take-off.

Flight engineers would also find themselves actively involved with the problems that beset the 747's early Pratt & Whitney engines. 'Because the engines were mainly the responsibility of the [flight engineer], he had to be vigilant at all times,' recalls Colin Lock. It was the engineer who had to manage the frequent engine stalls or surges at various times: during start-up, acceleration, thrust reduction on cruise or during descent, or even when using reverse thrust after landing. A close watch also had to be kept on the often-excessive oil usage by the early engines, which reminded some older flight engineers of what they termed their 'oil-usage nightmares' in the days of the Lockheed Constellations.

But the bogeyman was the 'wet' take-off where, to allow increased thrust for such long-range sectors such as Perth to Bombay or Bombay to London, demineralised water was injected into the engines to keep their turbine temperatures down. So while such long stage lengths might have improved the route economics, it also meant malfunctions were not uncommon, and there was always the risk of engine failure on one or even two engines. 'From memory, there were about eight scenarios, or permutations, of what could go wrong, and consequently it was generally a tense time for the flight engineer whenever a "wet" take-off was used,' says Lock.

Norm King too has memories of converting from the 707 to the 747:

If a non-threatening problem arose on the 707 for which there was no operations manual procedure, much was left to the initiative of the crew to work it out, with many of the problems resolved based on the intimate knowledge the flight engineer had of the systems. It was a source of professional pride to be able to accurately diagnose a defect in order to help the next station's ground engineer to fix it.

But the 747 was totally different when it came to operational philosophy. Now the 'book' was required for everything, and the way it was flown and operated was highly standardised, so the engineers often felt they had lost much of their ability to use their initiative and systems knowledge. 'I understood the reasons for this, with the 747 being a much more complicated beast than its predecessor,' King acknowledges. 'And naturally, therefore, Boeing wanted it to be safe in the hands of whomever might be the lowest common denominator to operate it!'

Thus, as his colleague Colin Lock describes it, flight engineers were no longer hands-on engineers. Although a good knowledge of the aircraft was required, and accurate troubleshooting was necessary, Boeing had developed a new system: when a defect occurred, the appropriate codes were transmitted over the radio and a maintenance engineer on the ground consulted a manual to diagnose the problem. As they watched such technology develop, many flight engineers realised the end of their place in the cockpit could not be too far away.

***

By the early 1980s, Qantas was beginning to show interest in the twin-engine Boeing 767, designed for a two-pilot crew. In some respects, the issue was a rerun of what had taken place on the domestic airline front almost two decades before, when the Department of Civil Aviation, despite efforts by the flight engineers' union, decreed that the DC-9 could operate in Australia with only a two-pilot crew.

In the case of the 767, however, its introduction was not quite so straightforward. Boeing first offered it with either a two- or a three-person cockpit layout. Responding to union pressure, Ansett ordered its 767s with an engineer's position and was the only airline to do so. In the case of Qantas, however, despite strong submissions from the flight engineers' union, the company ordered a two-pilot 767, with the compromise that flight engineers would be guaranteed employment until they retired from the airline.

Looking back at the 767 flight engineer issue, however, it's interesting to note the view of Qantas chief executive Keith Hamilton. As far as the airline's flight engineers were concerned, Hamilton suggested that they would continue to be utilised long into the future on the 747 fleet. 'It would then take many years for 21 existing B747s to be rolled over for new types and additional B747 aircraft would be added to accommodate increased traffic,' he noted in an internal memo. 'The Boeing Company have advised that the new 747-400 will be built to accommodate a three-man crew.'

The -400 would eventually roll off the Boeing assembly line accommodating a two-pilot crew. Although the flight engineers did not know it at the time, at least one version of their venerable 747 would play its part in extending their time in Qantas cockpits for several years. That version was the

-300 Classic, which Lock notes 'remained in service a lot longer than it was ever anticipated . . . In fact it had survived long enough to see off the first of the original Boeing B767s [that] departed the Qantas fleet in June 2003.'

By 2009, however, it was all over for flight engineers on Qantas long-haul flights. The last of the Classics left Sydney on 20 January, on a one-way flight to Marana in the Arizona desert, where it would eventually be broken up.

On arrival at Marana, flight engineer Rob Watt signed a nostalgic—and genuine—'Nil Defects' into the aircraft's technical log, and, as Colin Lock records, added an addendum:

This is the end,
Beautiful friend
This is the end.

It was, says Lock, 'Probably the best compliment you could give to the Qantas engineering staff and the Boeing Aircraft Corporation.'

20
'LUCK'S A FORTUNE'

Throughout aviation history, certain aircraft have left a lasting memory across whole generations of the travelling public, particularly when it comes to safety. Several, like the Douglas DC-3, attained iconic status before they passed the baton onto their international counterparts, like the Lockheed Constellation. With the jet era came the popular 707s and DC-8s, while others, like the de Havilland Comet, were involved in accidents that limited the success they may have otherwise known.

While comparisons between different aviation eras can be misleading, it is clear that the Boeing 747 established one of the most enviable reputations for safety in the eyes of air travellers. For those with long memories, however, there was one horrific exception. In March 1977, on Tenerife, in the Canary Islands off the west coast of Africa, there was an accident that everyone had hoped would never happen in the era of big passenger jets. In the worst disaster in aviation history,

583 people died when a KLM 747 and a Pan American 747 collided on Tenerife's runway.

Neither aircraft was scheduled to be there at all. Both had been diverted to Tenerife when a bomb planted by separatists of the Canary Islands Independence Movement exploded at Las Palmas airport on the island of Gran Canaria, their original destination. When they were finally cleared to resume their flights late in the afternoon of 27 March, the combination of limited runway visibility, and poor and confused communications between the control tower and the aircraft themselves, led to a situation where the KLM jumbo began its take-off roll while the Pan Am 747 was still taxiing on part of the runway.

The catastrophic result created a media frenzy that targeted airlines around the world. Qantas was no exception, with questions being asked about whether it could happen in Australia. In the rash of feature articles and television segments that followed the accident, the airline's safety reputation would, like that of hundreds of other Boeing operators, be held up to scrutiny. Within 48 hours of the accident, a request arrived at Qantas from the Sydney *Daily Telegraph* for one of the newspaper's feature writers to observe what went on in the cockpit of a 747 on a typical international sector.

Confident of its safety record, Qantas was quick to respond, offering a journalist a ride in the 'jump' seat behind the two-pilot crew on the Sydney–Perth sector of its next day's regular flight to South Africa. Several significant surprises were in store for the journalist, the first coming even before he'd witnessed the take-off.

Boarding through the terminal concourse, the writer arrived in the cockpit as the last of the passengers were coming aboard, surprised to find that the captain was the only one there. The first officer, the captain pointed out, was doing the 'walk around' of the aircraft on the tarmac outside, making sure everything was in order and all those working parts visible from the outside had no obvious obstructions. The journalist was in for his second surprise when the first officer finally arrived in the cockpit, took up his right-hand seat, turned to the captain and introduced himself. Was this first acquaintance staged for his benefit, the journalist wondered? After all, Qantas was at the time one of the world's smaller airlines.

From there, through pushback from the terminal, the long taxi and take off to Perth, followed by three and a half hours of chitchat about the life of an international airline pilot, things were pretty uneventful. Then, since another crew was rostered to take the aircraft on from Perth to Johannesburg, the captain invited the writer to follow through with any questions he might have over evening drinks at their Perth hotel.

Predictably, the journalist's opening gambit was to question how two crew members of such a relatively small airline had never met or flown with each other before that morning. With just the hint of a smile on his face, the captain offered an explanation. 'No, we may never have met before but I can tell you I know exactly how he flies,' he said. 'It's according to what we refer to as "the Qantas book". He also knows exactly how I fly and it's because of that book that we are only too ready to speak up when we think the other might be operating outside the procedures that book requires.'

The captain felt no need to explain further. The safety and training philosophy behind the operational procedures outlined in the metaphorical book was, he believed, beyond question. In the end, for Qantas, the article in the *Daily Telegraph* was a welcome attempt to reassure passengers of the safety of the 747 itself, and that they were in good hands in the air.

Before long, the Tenerife accident and the general subject of airline disasters slipped from the front pages and things returned to normal. Yet three subsequent incidents involving Qantas would show the airline just how fragile that normal could be. The first was over Germany, and the latter two—one in the air and another on the ground—occurred in Thailand. All three would test the boundaries of the airline's luck—and its reputation.

***

Qantas captain Fred Phillips had flown in German airspace for most of his life in aviation. Originally, he'd tangled nightly with the Luftwaffe as a master bomber with the RAF's Pathfinder Force. In 1977, again at night, he was about to tangle with them again.

Climbing out of Frankfurt and heading for Bahrain, Phillips had just passed 30,000 feet when the German air traffic controller warned him that his radar showed a batch of unidentified aircraft, apparently straying out of military airspace and heading in Phillips's direction. Still climbing through the last scattering of cloud, Phillips could do nothing but wait anxiously as the controller, still attempting to contact the miscreant aircraft, gave him several more reports, each confirming they were still 'closing' on him.

Within seconds of the controller's last alert, Phillips' 747 broke cloud to see German fighters flash past in the opposite direction on both sides of his aircraft, the closest one only a few hundred metres away. Phillips would later confess: 'All I could do was hang on and hope they'd miss.' He was even less impressed some weeks later when he received a letter from a Luftwaffe general explaining that 'such risks are the price we pay for keeping the peace in the Cold War'.

Thirteen years later, Qantas would experience a similarly dismissive response by a military commander, this time follow-ing another near miss over Asia. Like Fred Phillips' incident, it would be all over in seconds, but the near miss involving a Qantas 747-400 over Thailand would for years to come send shudders through many of the airline's operations staff.

It was just after 7 p.m. on 13 September 1990, and captain Geoff Westwood's flight QF10 operating from London to Sydney was cruising in scattered cloud at 37,000 feet in the early darkness, about to begin a gradual descent into Singa-pore. There Westwood and his crew would pass the last sector on to Sydney to a new crew.

Suddenly, without any warning, Westwood's entire cockpit windscreen was filled by the shape of another aircraft, flying across his aircraft's nose. There was no time to react and within seconds the bow wave from the intruder rolled the Boeing into a 15-degree tilt to the left. Westwood would later estimate the other aircraft—a United States Air Force Lockheed C5-A Galaxy freighter, one of the world's largest jets—had passed within 15 metres of his Boeing. Any closer and it would have almost certainly taken the tail off the 747.

Later studies of the 747's state-of-the-art flight management system would show just how fortunate QF10's passengers and crew had been that night. The flight management system, which allows the Boeing autopilot's altimeter settings to select the precise altitude the aircraft will fly at, can be engaged from either the captain's or the first officer's instrument panel. Even with such sophisticated equipment, there can be a difference of altitude depending on which system is chosen. On QF10 that night it had been Westwood who had set the altitude on his side of the cockpit. Tests showed that if the first officer's system had been chosen instead, their 747 would have been flying 50 feet higher, with disastrous consequences.

While Westwood and his shaken crew resumed the descent into Singapore, their military intruder continued east towards its US Air Force base at Honolulu, apparently none the wiser about the near miss. That was not the case in Qantas, however, and immediately Westwood received word that the airline's safety chief in Sydney, Ken Lewis, was on the phone to Honolulu to ask for an explanation as to why the Galaxy had been there in the first place.

'Well, there's a war on, you know,' was the base commanding officer's response.

Never one to take a backwards step, Lewis countered: 'I know that. I just didn't realise we were the enemy!'

Later, the US would claim that the Lockheed had attempted to contact Thai air traffic control but received no response and had therefore come into Thai airspace at the wrong altitude. The Thais, on the other hand, claimed they had no idea the aircraft was there.

Several weeks later, obviously as an attempt at appeasement, two US lieutenant colonels arrived at Lewis's office where what Lewis describes as 'a healthy exchange' took place. Nothing much happened after that, a situation that Lewis attributes to Iraq's Operation Desert Storm, which was underway at the time. The US military clearly had other priorities.

Nine years later, in 1999, Thailand again would be the scene of an incident, this time ending with the embarrassing sight of a giant Qantas 747 dug into the soft earth on the edge of a golf course.

***

From an airline's point of view, it is fortunate if an incident or accident results in no injuries or loss of life. But it's not ideal to have your aircraft feature every night on television as it sits bogged up to its wheels at the end of a runway. Numerous such embarrassments have occurred over the years and, sensitive to having a damaged aircraft sit with its name and logo in full view of the media and the public, airlines have adopted a variety of tactics to dilute the impact of such unfortunate displays.

In Australia, one of the most memorable examples occurred in December 1969 when a Pan Am 707 suffered a bird strike while taking off for Honolulu on Sydney's north–south runway. Unable to abandon the take-off in time, the 707 ended up stuck firmly in the soil at the northern end of the runway, in plain sight of the main access road to the international terminal. With no chance of it being moved for many hours, it didn't take long for Pan Am's engineers to reduce their airline's embarrassment by dropping the 707's tail fin sideways to obscure the Pan Am logo. Pan Am may have given a reason for it—that its height was causing an obstruction to the use of the runway, for example—but the move certainly helped limit damage to the airline's image.

Unfortunately for Pan Am, they couldn't repeat the tail-fin manoeuvre two years later when, while landing on the airport's east–west runway, one of their 747s again overran, this time ending up just short of large concrete service pipes. Rather than seeking to exploit each other's embarrassments, however, airlines generally have a healthy regard for that old saying: 'There but for the grace of God go I.'

On that September night in 1999 over Thailand, heavy rain and limited visibility confronted Qantas's flagship service QF1 as it approached Bangkok. Ahead of them, unbeknown to the pilots of QF1, the crew of another of the airline's Boeing 747s, QF15, had already abandoned their initial landing approach and were in the process of circling around for another attempt.

QF1's first officer was flying the plane, and only seconds before touchdown the captain told him to abandon the landing and go around, because the rain was so heavy and visibility so poor. As the report of the incident later revealed, just as the first officer pushed the thrust levers forward, the 747's wheels touched the runway and the captain pulled off the thrust.

What followed was, as is the case in most aviation accidents, a confluence of factors that worked against QF1 and its safe landing. Most significantly, the aircraft was still travelling too fast and, to add to the crew's woes, the deluge of rain on the runway was causing the wheels to aquaplane, thus severely limiting the stopping power of the brakes.

The end result was the more than 300-tonne QF-1 rolling off the end of the runway, its wheels driving into the ground just a nine iron's shot from the boundary of the surrounding golf course. Fortunately for Qantas, although the incident would be one of the most embarrassing in its history, there were no casualties beyond some red faces throughout the company. Recovering the Boeing so that Bangkok, one of Asia's busiest transit points, could return to normal was also a Herculean task.

Even after the Boeing had been cleared from the airport, the accident itself continued to have consequences for the airline. In a desperate attempt to lessen the ongoing damage to its reputation, Qantas initially adopted what one journalist described as 'a cat-and-mouse game' with the media to even avoid revealing where in Asia the Boeing was being repaired. Hiding something the size of a Boeing 747 from public view wouldn't prove the easiest of assignments for the airline, though. Several Australian media outlets launched determined efforts to find the aircraft, which resulted in the whole sorry saga being in the news for far longer than it needed to be.

Even the airline's chief executive, James Strong, tried to put the best possible spin on the affair. In one subsequent television interview, he resorted to referring to Bangkok as an 'incident' rather than an 'accident', a description that hardly fitted the background image of QF1 up to its axles in mud. News outlets estimated the eventual cost of repairs at around $100 million but Qantas was careful not to reveal the actual figure.

As is often the case on such occasions, though, humour was never far from the surface. Only weeks into his new role as executive manager of aircraft operations, David Forsyth completed an agonising series of media interviews about the accident. Shortly afterwards, his secretary received a phone call from an elderly woman who explained that she was a long-term Qantas customer who had been on QF1 and then insisted she be put through to talk to Forsyth.

'I was on it when it ran off the runway,' the customer told Forsyth, 'and I just want you to know that I will continue to fly with Qantas because it always has safe accidents!'

21

THE HUMOUR
OF IT ALL

If there is one word that has continued to identify Qantas to the general public, from the days of Avro 504 and Hudson Fysh to the Boeing 747 era, it is safety. The airline's safety culture would earn it world renown, and there could be no compromises.

Safety brings with it a heavy responsibility, but scratch the surface and beneath this essential culture lay another very Australian trait: a vibrant sense of humour, not only providing the odd laugh but occasionally easing the tension in what is a very serious business. Such a situation is not exclusive to Qantas and can be seen across the whole spectrum of Australian aviation—and often on the most unlikely occasions. Take, for example, Lae, Papua New Guinea, in the mid-1960s.

An RAF Hastings transport aircraft transiting from the British base at Honiara in the Solomon Islands had declared an emergency as it approached Lae, the first stop on its way home to the UK. Airport emergency vehicles were on standby, but the Hastings touched down safely and taxied towards Lae's small passenger terminal, where the local airport manager walked out to meet the crew. He was standing under the wing as the Hastings' captain, a flight lieutenant, came around to join him.

'What happened, skipper?' the manager asked, a quizzical frown on his face at the branches and small twigs protruding from the lower wing and engine nacelles.

'We had a bird strike and I think it might have fouled the hydraulics,' was the reply.

Renowned for his wit, the manager continued staring upwards: 'Christ, mate, were they still in the trees?'

What had in fact occurred was patently obvious. The Hastings' traditional flypast farewell, common when crews were returning home after a posting to South Pacific shores, had stayed a fraction too low for too long and cleaned up the tops of trees off the end of Honiara's runway. The damage was easily fixed and the Hastings was soon on its way again, presumably with the flight lieutenant having some explaining to do when he reached squadron headquarters in the UK.

***

While the RAF flight lieutenant probably couldn't be cast in this category, in the case of Qantas there were occasionally those who would win respect throughout the airline for a willingness to make light of an otherwise serious situation. Take captain Les Hayward, whose long Qantas 747 career ranged from moments of high drama to occasions when he was only too willing to tell a joke against himself.

Hayward won a degree of respect from many in the airline for the front-line role he played in the bitter cabin crew industrial dispute that marked the entry of the 747 SP's introduction in January 1981. At one stage, he remembers, he was spat upon and, by his own account, 'roughed up a bit' while acting as a decoy to avoid any confrontation between male members of the striking cabin crew and the female flight attendants who had agreed to keep flying.

But he still manages a wry smile when he recounts a series of incidents during his long career with Qantas, including a brief brush with the law in Melbourne.

It was mid-March 1978 and the day had not started well for Hayward. While he was approaching Tullamarine on the first sector of his QF7 Sydney–Melbourne–Perth flight, Melbourne's weather suddenly deteriorated to the point where he was considering returning the aircraft to Sydney. Urgent discussions between Hayward, Qantas Melbourne and air traffic control, however, came up with an alternative: he should divert instead to Avalon, near Geelong, and passengers from Melbourne would be bussed there to join the flight.

The rapid rearrangements worked without a hitch and QF7 was 'buttoned up' and about to resume its flight to Perth when a van load of Victorian police arrived unannounced and ordered all passengers off again. Several hours earlier, three jewellery merchants had been shot dead in an execution-style robbery on the eighth floor of Melbourne's Manchester Unity

Building. Police now wanted to ensure the culprits weren't trying to leave the country on Hayward's QF7, but their investigation would not be as straightforward as they might have wished.

Complications began when the police contingent announced they intended to search the passengers who had been bussed from Melbourne. Hayward's 747 was ultimately destined for Athens, and most of the Greek passengers already onboard refused to cooperate. It wasn't until Hayward stepped in to talk to one of them that their reason became clear.

'It turned out many were small shopkeepers who were carrying large amounts of cash—on which tax had probably not been paid—and certainly more than an amount normally allowed for export,' Hayward recalls. 'When I explained this to the police chief, he announced in Greek they were looking for jewellery not cash and ensured them any cash found would be ignored. That finally solved the problem.'

After several hours checking with no result, the police left and QF7 was once again on its way to Perth. Unfortunately for Hayward, his problems weren't over. On approach to Perth, in darkness, the airport runway lights failed. Quickly alerting the RAAF that he might have to divert to their base at Pearce, Hayward was just about to turn the 747 northwards when the runway lights flashed on again.

After a break in Perth it was on to Damascus the next day, where Hayward's 'nightmarish trip' would continue. Due to repairs being carried out on Damascus's regular arrivals runway, Hayward would be required to land instead on the runway being used for departing aircraft. This was not really a major problem but it would require his jumbo to execute a 180-degree turn at the end of the runway to taxi back towards the terminal.

It wasn't until he reached the end of his landing run that Hayward discovered the normal turning bay at its end was also under repair and unusable, which forced him to attempt to turn the jumbo within the narrow width of the runway itself. The manoeuvre resulted in the 300-tonne jumbo falling around a metre short, and it ended up sitting at right angles to the runway—thus effectively closing the airport.

After repeated attempts to call for towing assistance and with a sandstorm restricting visibility, Hayward, with vivid memories of the disastrous KLM/Pan Am accident at Tenerife in the 1970s, attempted to use reverse thrust on the jumbo's engines to execute a three-point turn. While this emergency technique was possible with the more tolerant engines of the Boeing 707, such was not the case with the far more complex power plants of the 747. The result was significant damage to the engines.

Some days later, finally back in Perth on the return journey and with the horrors of the trip behind him, Hayward could have been forgiven for having a sense of relief when he accepted an invitation to do a publicity interview for Qantas on Perth radio station 6PR. Hayward had no idea the invitation was part of a plot and therefore suspected nothing when his first officer Peter Blair-Hickman declined to accompany him. Blair-Hickman suggested the second officer go instead.

Midway through the interview, the radio presenter announced that while normally his program didn't do talkback radio, that day they would make an exception. With that he introduced his first caller, who introduced himself as 'Mr Amity'. The caller already knew how a pilot turned an aircraft as large as a 747 around in the air, he said, 'but how do you do it on the ground?'

'Mr Amity told me I could call him Cal, but even then the penny still didn't drop,' Hayward confesses. It was not until the following day, midway through the flight back to Sydney, that Peter Blair-Hickman slipped out of the cockpit for a break and, using the interphone in the galley and the same voice as the previous day, called the flight deck and advised Hayward that 'Cal Amity is calling!'

'For the remainder of my days in Qantas, my nickname was "Captain Calamity",' Hayward chuckles.

The fact that he can still laugh as he tells such stories offers an insight into the way that many pilots in the 747 era could enliven the often boring yet sometimes extremely serious and tense hours in the cockpit with a joke against others or themselves.

***

Long-time captains like Gordon Power will tell you that Les Hayward was not alone in inheriting a colourful or cutting nickname among those who flew the 747 line. But in keeping with human nature, there were contrasts.

Some pilots could be among the most pleasant individuals you would meet anywhere but their demeanour would instantly change the moment they entered the aircraft. Marsh Burgess, says Power, was one such pilot. 'The rest of the crew would sit on the edge of their seats for the whole flight waiting to see who would be next in line for a tongue lashing,' he remembers. 'My wife once told me she knew when I had been flying with Marsh as she couldn't talk to me for days afterwards!'

In an industry susceptible to nicknames, Burgess earned the nom de plume 'Harpic' or 'Round-the-Bend', but this took nothing away from his ability as a pilot. On one occasion, flying in Papua New Guinea, he had landed his Catalina flying boat in rough seas in the Papuan Gulf and saved the life of a lone yachtsman.

Power recalls yet another captain, who had earned an equally characterful nickname. At the time Gowings Department store in Sydney was renowned for serving the clothing needs of the average working man, offering everything from tailored trousers to a well-known pair of braces labelled 'Police and Firemen'. At 'slip' ports around the world it was normal procedure for Qantas crews to receive a call from their hotel's desk around 45 minutes before their flights, to ensure they would be ready for the crew bus to the airport. The staff of one hotel in Teheran, one of the first such points after leaving London, often made mistakes and failed to call crew members. When that happened to the traffic officer on this particular captain's flight, he suspended him on the spot. From then onwards the captain bore the nickname 'Police and Firemen The Universal Suspender'.

***

Thanks to their surrounding terrain, many of the world's international airports have their idiosyncrasies, whether it be the vicious crosswinds of New Zealand's Wellington or the uneven surface of Greece's Athens. But before it was replaced by the more benign surroundings of Chek Lap Kok, Hong Kong's Kai Tak was among the most demanding places to land an airliner. Even a newly appointed Qantas captain often had to wait six months before being approved to operate there, with even that first arrival being under the close scrutiny of a check captain. So conscious were pilots of Kai Tak's demands that one newly appointed captain adopted a practice similar to many professional golfers who 'walk the course' before a major tournament. In his case, the pilot walked the streets along Kai Tak's approach path to experience it from ground level.

Rated as the sixth most dangerous airport in the world, Kai Tak was located on the west side of Hong Kong's Kowloon Bay. The area was surrounded not only by mountains but, thanks to Hong Kong's acute residential demands, up to six-storey apartment buildings so close to the planes that any sharp-eyed passengers looking out the window could see television sets in the apartments as their jumbos passed by.

From a pilot's viewpoint, this was no straightforward approach down a gentle glide slope provided by the technology of an instrument landing system. Rather bizarrely in the aviation context, it was instead a case of pointing the 747 towards a large red-and-white-painted chequerboard sign on the side of a hill. At this point the captain, looking across the cockpit at right angles from his left-hand seat, would get a view of the runway through the first officer's window and begin to manually fly the aircraft through a 90-degree turn to line up with the runway. From there, the pilot had 30 seconds to touchdown. As one senior captain once put it, 'If you achieved a good landing at Hong Kong you walked away very pleased with yourself.'

Of course, the others in the cockpit also had grandstand seats for this landing phenomenon, and Norm King has lasting memories of his first trip into Hong Kong as flight engineer. He tells the story with his renowned sense of humour. 'Kai Tak was either the best bang for your buck or infamous for its degree of difficulty, depending on the personality type of the person you were speaking to,' King remembers. 'So naturally, with all the talk about how the crew had to be at the top of their game to come out of Hong Kong alive, I did all the homework I could before leaving on that trip. I needed to be as prepared as I could for this supposedly highly hazardous approach and landing.'

To add to the drama of it all, when the day arrived for Norm King's Kai Tak initiation, his captain in command just happened to bear the nickname of '006½', 'so-called because he was in the style of James Bond but not yet quite up to that exalted level . . . nevertheless I was expecting him to exercise the greatest flying skills I'd be ever likely to see.'

'Not uncommon in those days, his first action was to pull on a pair of white kid gloves as we pass through about 5000 feet on approach, where the buildings are getting bigger. So far so good, but the next thing he does is to light up not a cigarette, but a cigar.' As a result, says King, visibility on the flight deck decreased significantly as the notorious Checkerboard Hill came into view:

> It's at about this point that our captain takes the handset from the rear of the centre console, props it between his tilted head and right shoulder and, using his chin on the 'push-to-talk' button, begins to describe the passing scenery of nearby buildings for his passengers.
>
> By now he is holding the cigar in his right hand while wrestling the control column using his left and eventually the huge chequerboard completely fills the view out of the flight-deck windows.
>
> The last-minute right turn to line up with the runway is executed perfectly and with a few subtle control inputs '006½' greases it on without even a trace of cigar ash falling off the now much shorter cheroot. So much for the dreaded approach to Kai Tak!

***

Just as pilots and flight engineers could see humour even as they battled the vagaries of airport approaches, cabin crew attending to the needs of the hundreds of passengers on a Boeing 747 could also see the funny side.

Former cabin crew member Peter McLaughlan recalls one female passenger on a Honolulu–Sydney flight complaining loudly about the fact that by the time the meal trolley arrived at her seat it had run out of the seafood meal. Although slightly miffed at the passenger's performance, when the crew member in charge of the galley eventually located another seafood plate he decided to deliver it himself. So, unpacking the scuba diving kit he had purchased while on his Honolulu layover and donning his wetsuit, mask, snorkel and flippers, he set off down the aisle carrying a tray above his head and announcing at the top of his voice: 'Who ordered the fish?'

McLaughlan also tells of another occasion when a rude passenger in economy, more than a little under the weather, wrinkled his nose at the meal tray put in front of him. 'You can take this away, mate,' he declared. 'This meal isn't fit for a pig.'

'Certainly, sir,' said the steward, who had already dealt with too many problems created by this particular passenger. 'I'll go and get you one that is.'

Then there was what became known as the case of 'the body in Bahrain'.

With millions of people travelling around the world on 747s each year, the occasional death does occur on board. On a flight to Athens in December 1971, a terminally ill female passenger, accompanied by her husband and a doctor, was hoping to reach Greece before she died but passed away between Singapore and Kuala Lumpur. Cabin crews are trained to be aware of the delicacy of such situations and, after seeking the approval of other passengers, arrangements were made to borrow a stretcher from the BOAC agent in Kuala Lumpur and have the deceased laid out across a row of seats in the rearmost section of the 747.

Under normal circumstances, this would create no difficulties during any further stops en route to Greece, but on this occasion things became more complicated for flight service director Dave Cohen. At the next stop, Bahrain, the 747's arrival was planned to be part of the pomp and ceremony of the opening of Bahrain's new international terminal building. Although Qantas competitor airline BOAC had contributed several million dollars to the construction of the new terminal, thanks to the timing of the arrival of the Qantas flight it would be Cohen's 747, not a BOAC one, that would be inspected by the Emir of Bahrain as part of the opening ceremony.

So, even with all passengers unloaded and the recently deceased passenger out of sight in the rear section, the Emir's inspection would require Cohen to exercise a mixture of diplomatic finesse and white lies, particularly when, during his inspection, the Emir inquired of Cohen whether it was true someone on board was 'quite ill'.

'Yes—but she's much better now,' Cohen told him. Now long retired, Cohen still remains convinced that BOAC Kuala Lumpur had not only loaned him the stretcher but, miffed at the fact that Qantas would steal their thunder in Bahrain, had tipped off the Emir's party about the circumstances on board.

With that exchange behind him, Cohen encouraged the Emir to inspect the upstairs lounge and cockpit, only to be confronted with a second problem when, as he followed Cohen up the 747's spiral stairway to the lounge, the Emir accidentally jammed his ceremonial sword in its railings.

'When he released it and passed it up to me, his two burly bodyguards moved quickly up behind him in my direction, presumably worried about what I might do with it!' says Cohen, who confesses it made that particular flight one of the more interesting experiences of his long Qantas career.

***

Not that those flying with Qantas on 747s were the only ones to see the funny side of some of their problems, even when it came to the inherent dangers involved in dealing with the likes of the airline's chairmen—and one of them in particular.

No one could seriously credit Sir Lenox Hewitt with displaying much humour during his five years as chairman in the 1970s. Nor could anyone match his ability to instil fear in the hearts of those serving in Qantas's overseas ports. An inveterate traveller during his time with the airline, with an overseas itinerary far exceeding any of his predecessors as chairman, Hewitt's frequent trips prompted some executives, like Queensland region marketing man Brian Kirkham, to adopt the practice of sending alerts in the form of telex messages to warn Qantas people that the formidable Hewitt was headed their way.

Kirkham's telexes, famously headed 'Our gain is your loss', not only created folklore in their own right, but served as a timely warning for what could often be an unsettling experience for overseas staff. Nor was it unusual for Hewitt's abrasive personality to generate its own brand of wry humour among those at home in Australia, one primary example coming after a Hewitt initiative to 'encourage' the airline to carry meat to the Middle East at $1.10 per kilogram, a rock-bottom price.

For this minimal cost, meat exporters were able to consign their meat from Sydney, Melbourne, Brisbane or Perth via Qantas flights to Bahrain, where a staff member based there would oversee transshipment via Gulf Air to eight other Middle Eastern ports: Damascus, Kuwait, Dubai, Abu Dhabi, Muscat, Dhahran, Jeddah and Riyadh. It all looked extremely good on paper, particularly to New Zealanders, who quickly moved to increase their beef supply to the Australian market.

Watching the economics of it all, it didn't take long for the miffed Qantas cargo people to suggest a new nickname for their chairman: 'A Dollar Ten Len'.

And their chairman's tendency to make unannounced raids on Qantas's Mascot cargo terminal could also bring problems, particularly on one holiday weekend. A young Australian tourist had been killed in a motorcycle accident in Bali, and Hewitt found out that the tourist's body, in its coffin, was being stored in the warehouse racking.

One of the first phone calls that cargo manager Norm Leek received on his return to work on Tuesday morning was from Hewitt demanding to know why he had 'no respect for the relatives of the dead'. Leek's investigation revealed that although the undertaker had been advised of the arrival of the coffin on the Saturday morning, his response had been: 'Well, as he's not going anywhere over the holiday weekend, we'll collect him on Tuesday.'

In typical Hewitt fashion, the chairman then demanded to 'see the file', which presented Leek with a further problem: he didn't have one. So a brief one was quickly concocted comprising a dummy 'air waybill', along with a note recording the telephone exchange with the undertaker, but even that didn't satisfy Hewitt. 'Mr Leek, you have the audacity to call that a file?'

'Thank goodness when I assured him that was all I had, I never heard any more,' says Leek.

Leek recalls another problem with a booklet produced during Hewitt's time as chairman as part of a 747 marketing campaign aimed at inspiring young Australians to travel overseas. Entitled *The First Attempt to Get You to Leave the Country*, the booklet contained humorous travel anecdotes and clever cartoons matched with helpful advice, and was designed to be sold through booking offices and travel agents. It created a lot of interest—which, unfortunately, led to Hewitt asking a senior marketing manager how many copies had been sold.

'Thousands,' was the quick reply, and Hewitt insisted on seeing the evidence. His demand sent immediate panic through the accounting ranks: no such tally existed. 'Marketing staff then spent most of one night creating bodgie marketing receipts to match the "ballpark" figure,' Leek admits. 'When it came to the chairman and our marketing people, there was never a dull moment.'

22
NOT JUST ANY PASSENGERS

Beyond the often slick television commercials showcasing its smiling cabin crew and tempting in-flight service en route to exotic international holiday destinations, there existed a very different Qantas 747. It was one that former chief executive John Ward once summed up as 'an extensive airlift capacity and engineering capability to support defence and emergency services'.

Behind that rather bland description are numerous stories of an airline at the forefront of emergencies in Australia's recent history. From the tragic devastation of weather events to the rescue of Australians from areas of sudden political turmoil, Qantas 747s have provided the speed and versatility of an aeroplane that no other form of transport is capable of matching.

When it comes to weather disasters in Australia, the most dramatic in living memory occurred on Christmas Eve 1974 when Cyclone Tracy ripped Darwin apart. Younger generations may not have experienced the drama of Darwin's destruction almost 50 years ago, but a few simple statistics capture the havoc caused by torrential rain and wind gusts of up to 217 kilometres per hour: at least 65 people died, with sixteen of them missing at sea; only 400 of the city's 10,000 buildings remained intact; and 35 vessels of varying sizes in Darwin's harbour were either sunk or run aground. Within the space of several hours a town of more than 40,000 people had no water or electricity, in a remote location far from the help of the rest of the country.

The first aircraft into Darwin was a TAA Fokker Friendship, which was soon followed on that Christmas Day by a Qantas 707 bringing medical staff, other personnel and equipment, and a single sideband radio that would connect Darwin to the rest of Australia, helping to coordinate a rescue uplift that would create its own records.

The next morning, Boxing Day, captain John Brooks, his 707 loaded with patients chosen by a medical team, took off for Sydney carrying 266 passengers, more than twice the Boeing's normal load. Some sat on other people's laps, or on the floor. Other records would be shattered in the days that followed as RAAF Hercules transports and an assortment of other aircraft began carrying supplies in and people out. Without any critical facilities operating, Darwin needed to be stripped of its population as quickly as possible, at least until essential services could return.

Memories of that Christmas still linger with those who took part, one of whom was Qantas medical department nurse Marita Wilkinson. Not only did she arrive onboard John Brooks's 707, but she returned three days later to assist in the evacuation onboard a Qantas 747. 'It might have been eons ago now but every Christmas I remember Cyclone Tracy,' Wilkinson recalls.

She says that among the survivors the psychological trauma and the worries about an uncertain future were very clear to see.

The Qantas medical team on the ground had already attended to the injured before boarding the flights and by now it was obvious that the reality of that devastating storm had had time to sink in for the evacuees. There were no bandaid solutions here, only talking, offering reassurance and sharing a laugh could provide a relief to many. And among them were children who had never been on a plane before and here they were on this 'Big Bird'.

The Boeing 747 would make two return trips to Sydney that day, with one of the flights breaking a world record by carrying 673 passengers, several hundred more than its normal load. Qantas wasn't the only one breaking records either. Flight lieutenant John Pickett's aircraft was just one of the RAAF's C-130 Hercules that stretched the limits, carrying 179 passengers—twice its normal load.

Within ten days, the massive military and civilian air operation had lifted more than 20,000 people out of the

Northern Territory capital, a quarter of them by Qantas. But while the thousands displaced by Tracy worried about how to rebuild their lives and their devastated community, within a few weeks the world would be watching as another crisis unfolded, this time in Asia. Again, a Qantas 747 would prove its value in a humanitarian emergency.

***

It was early April 1975 and the long-running Vietnam War was entering its final tortuous days. By then, American and Australian troops had long gone, and military and civilian casualties were mounting daily as the North Vietnamese army drove relentlessly south until its ultimate destination, Saigon, was surrounded.

Unlike the two world wars and the Korean conflict that preceded it, the Vietnam War did not have widespread support. Since 1972 and the election of the Whitlam government, Australian involvement in Vietnam had declined to the point where even those attached to Australia's embassy were preparing to leave.

For Qantas, its role in the Vietnam War was now about to come full circle. In the early days of the war, its 707s had flown in Australian troops and returned them home at the end of their tour. Now it was being called upon to take part in what would be called Operation Babylift, one of the last humanitarian efforts of the war: a combined American and Australian operation between 4 and 18 April 1975 to carry war orphans out to adoptive families in the US and Australia.

Operation Babylift began with the efforts of Australian missionary Rosemary Taylor, who had been working with women and children at refugee camps in Vietnam, Cambodia and Thailand. As the situation in South Vietnam worsened, Taylor had been pressing Australian authorities to rescue the orphans who could be adopted by Australian families.

The first that most people in Australian heard about it was in early April, when prime minister Gough Whitlam announced that a Qantas Boeing 747 would leave that afternoon for Bangkok carrying 25 tonnes of supplies, including rice, milk powder and corned beef, as well as emergency relief. Also on board would be former diplomat and government minister Bill Morrison, and a medical team of doctors and nurses. There would be two Qantas charters, the first a 747 to Sydney and a subsequent 707 to Melbourne. Each would wait in Bangkok for two RAAF Hercules flights to bring 194 infants out of Saigon, some as babies packed aboard, the smallest of them in cardboard boxes on the floor.

The airlifts by US military aircraft carrying children to the United States did not start well. Soon after the first of the RAAF Hercules flew south-west towards Bangkok, tragedy struck when a US Air Force C-5A Galaxy freighter carrying 243 children, their escorts and medical staff crashed shortly after taking off from Saigon's Tan Son Nhut air base, killing 143 of the children and two Australian women who had volunteered to help on the flight.

By the time the RAAF Hercules arrived in Bangkok, the first of the Qantas charters was ready. The 747's upper-deck

Captain Cook lounge had been converted into an intensive care ward, and the smallest infants were placed head-to-toe in the cardboard boxes. Below them, forward of the front galley in B Zone, were other infants around six months old.

The uplift would leave a lasting impression on cabin crew air chef Ray Finn:

> C Zone had kids under one year old to whom we fastened our red-and-white crew tags around their hands or feet to record their seat location and noting the times they were fed or received treatment, with medical staff supervising us on how best to feed the children. That was okay until we ran out of baby formula and clean bottles, which meant we then had to resort to sterilising the bottles and filling them with watered down lemonade.

The medical condition of the children varied. Finn remembers one girl of about three years old who came on board severely dehydrated: 'She couldn't walk, talk or even smile but after several hours of feeding and close attention she was laughing and running around the aisles.'

Hers was one of the nicer stories, however. For much of the flight, the crew used whatever means they could to help children who were struggling to survive. At one stage, Qantas nurse Margaret Daly had to tear off her identity badge and use it to help fasten a breathing tube to a seat, while flight attendant Jenny Young spent the entire flight nursing a ten-day-old baby girl and a twelve-month-old boy, both suffering from trauma.

On arrival in Sydney, ambulances were waiting to rush the children to hospital. But the tired crew and nursing staff, who had worked non-stop throughout the flight, were left standing on the tarmac as they watched their transport take officials and press who had met the flight back to the terminal. Finn was not impressed. 'So after waiting a length of time we were left to walk,' he remembers. 'I still feel the medical staff did not receive due recognition for an outstanding job.'

The accompanying 707 charter encountered difficulties of its own. Before it could leave Bangkok, Thai authorities demanded that the names of the children be lodged before the aircraft would be allowed to depart. Faced with the fact that most of the infants didn't even have names, the 707's captain, Alan Bones, came up with his own solution: he gathered his cabin crew and suggested they compile their own 'Disney list'. Thus some children joined the flight as Mickey Mouse, Donald Duck and other Disney characters. When they ran out of Disneys, one was tagged Sydney H. Bridge.

After medical clearance, the children were offered for adoption, joining families across most Australian states. In 2001, many of them would join their cabin crew rescuers at a reunion at Mascot's Cabin Crew Centre. Several others sought out a 'Captain Bones' to thank him for their new lives in Australia.

***

Almost fifteen years later, a Qantas 747 charter was involved in another Asian crisis, this time wresting Australians in 1989 from what would become known as mainland China's 'June Fourth Incident', centred on Beijing's Tiananmen Square.

Reports at the time suggested several reasons for the protests by students, among them the poor state of the Chinese economy and claims of corruption within the Chinese Communist Party. By 5 June, television audiences across the world were witnessing soldiers converging on the square and other parts of Beijing, and using force to quell the riots. Among the most memorable images was a young man waving a bag to briefly stop several tanks from advancing across the square towards him.

Within 24 hours of that footage going to air, the Department of Foreign Affairs, concerned for the safety of around 400 Australians in Beijing and its surrounds, was calling Qantas to ask what capacity would be available for an evacuation. Soon after midnight on 7 June, a 747 under the command of captain Jim Dye was given clearance to break the Mascot curfew and be on its way, first to a fuelling and provisioning stop at Tokyo.

Behind Dye in the jumbo's cabin would be a unique team, with veteran flight service director Denis Liston leading a crew made up almost entirely of other flight service directors, along with a chief steward who happened to be in the crew office at Mascot at the time and volunteered to go along. Another of those on board, cabin crew security chief Bob Parker, recalls that in terms of years of service it would rank as one of the most senior crewing flights ever operated by his airline. 'Someone added up we had almost 400 years of service behind us,' says Parker. 'I know Denis had around 30 and I had 25.'

For the crews working on the flight, it would be a very different Beijing airport to the one they were accustomed to seeing on Qantas's normal weekly service. 'It was so strange to go into an airport with no one there beyond the few to meet us, and even the terminal itself in semi-darkness,' recalls Parker.

He remembers other differences: 'While all 373 passengers had boarding passes, none had allocated seat numbers, but I seem to remember we eventually took off with few children sitting on the floor!' For some it had been a last-minute scramble to make the flight, with one embassy staff member telling the ABC he had spent the whole morning tossing sensitive documents down the incinerator 'until I was literally tapped on the shoulder, told the buses were ready and didn't have time to change. I hopped on the bus and landed in Hong Kong still in my boilersuit.'

Others remember a very steep take-off, quickly explained by an announcement from the flight deck: 'Sorry about that but there was an armed gun emplacement at the runway and I didn't want to take any risks we didn't need to, so we're getting out of here as quickly as we can.' Said another passenger: 'I think many of my colleagues will tell you that we drank the plane dry by the time we got to Hong Kong.'

A second flight from Australia on 8 June lifted a further 390 passengers out of Shanghai, comprising many who had left the original flight in Hong Kong. In the near future, Shanghai itself would become a regular destination on the Qantas network.

***

Just over 30 years later, the 747 would be called again to rescue Australians stranded by a crisis in China. While this time there were no gunshots or tanks rolling across a city square, in early 2020 a very different danger presented itself when China's ninth-largest city, Wuhan, became the epicentre of a coronavirus outbreak which was about to spread across the world.

The Department of Foreign Affairs had identified a total of 243 Australians as 'prioritised and vulnerable and isolated' and requiring evacuation, 89 of them under sixteen years old and five younger than two. Again with an all-volunteer crew and with officials of the Department of Health, the 747 left Sydney around midday on Sunday, 2 February, and, after a brief stopover in Hong Kong, arrived in Wuhan late that night.

This was anything but a normal Qantas charter. Wuhan's locked-down airport was closed to all other traffic to allow for comprehensive passenger health protocols and immigration checks, and the Boeing remained on the ground for more than seven hours. That flight, and a subsequent one a week later direct to Darwin, were very unusual experiences for the Qantas crews, thanks to a number of precautions put in place to manage the risk of any transmission of the disease.

First, there was no sign of the normal Qantas onboard cabin service. Food and drinks for passengers had been placed on the seats before boarding to minimise crew contact. Beyond the safety requirement of manning the doors for departure and arrival, the crew, wearing masks and gloves, remained on the upper deck for most of the flight. Medical-grade filters specifically designed to remove particles in the air, including viruses, ensured new air was circulated into the cabin every five minutes as the aircraft headed for Exmouth on the Western Australian coast. From there, passengers were flown on RAAF aircraft to Christmas Island for a period of isolation.

Cabin services manager Brett Smith, who was on the second flight—first to Hong Kong, then Wuhan and Darwin—recalls how different this was to a normal Qantas operation. 'Since we didn't normally fly to Wuhan we had to take our own support crew, including our own ramp team, an engineer, check-in staff, Qantas medical as well as staff from Foreign Affairs and Border Force,' Smith explains. 'Because that group had previously operated the first relief flight to Wuhan they were considered a risk and therefore weren't allowed off the aircraft in Hong Kong, so they literally bunked down on board!'

Smith describes his first impression of locked-down Wuhan as 'like a scene out of a movie'. Its multi-lane highways, devoid of vehicles, gave it the appearance of a ghost town. 'One of the biggest challenges was the passenger boarding process which, for a 747, normally took about 45 minutes, but because of the social-distancing processes on this occasion took us six hours.'

There were differences too on the 747 itself, with the upper-deck business-class cabin reserved as a sterile area for the support crew, and the premium economy section below as a designated triage medical area in case anyone fell ill during the flight. With crew staying isolated from the passengers unless absolutely necessary, the airline's normal in-cabin service was also somewhat different to what Smith was used to.

'We were all masked up and the one thing we always took great pride in was our personal service style, but that had to go out the window too with limited interaction with passengers. I had to remind crew—no hugging, no touching arms, no holding babies, and it went against the grain of what we do, but we did our best to express our support from a distance.'

On landing in Darwin, they were gratified to receive a burst of applause from their passengers. 'Even if you couldn't see their faces behind their masks, you could see the appreciation in their eyes.' Despite his earlier experiences flying passengers on exclusive, three-week Qantas first-class tours around the world, Smith rates Wuhan among his more memorable experiences.

From Darwin, the passengers were transferred to the Howard Springs quarantine centre. So effective had the Qantas measures been to protect the crew themselves that none were required to quarantine after the flight. The same could not be said for the 747 itself, however, which was subjected to several days of deep cleaning on arrival back in Sydney.

Prime minister Scott Morrison and Qantas chief executive Alan Joyce later thanked the Chinese government for their cooperation with the complicated logistics of the flights. Joyce, who met the aircraft on arrival back in Sydney, also paid tribute to those involved: 'I'm so proud of our crews that they volunteered to do this, even though they knew there was a slight risk.'

There was one other notable aspect of the flights to Wuhan: they would be the last rescue flight missions to be carried out by Qantas 747s. Five months later, the type would forever leave Australian skies.

23
THE ANTARCTIC AIRLINE

As with many of his bold schemes, Dick Smith's idea to take Australians on sightseeing flights to the Antarctic came while he was looking at a map. It was 1977, and after putting together some estimates of distance and aircraft range, Smith—a man renowned for combining an adventurous bent with a passion for aviation firsts—realised that such a spectacular and unique travel destination as the south magnetic pole was within the range of a Boeing 707 return flight from Sydney without a refuelling stop.

Venturing into the southern polar regions wasn't particularly new in aviation. Indeed, it was Lan Chile that claimed the first commercial experiment back in 1956 when one of their DC-6Bs, with 66 passengers on board, ventured over the South Shetland Islands and Trinity Peninsula. Beyond that, aviation in the region had mostly been missions to support Antarctic activities by countries with bases there.

Qantas 707s had occasionally skipped across the edges of the Antarctic, mainly on charters between Australia and South America.

When Smith first mentioned his idea of a sightseeing tour of the white continent, Qantas took some convincing but were gradually persuaded—provided that Smith could fill the whole aeroplane himself. So, for Smith, it was back to the economics. His calculations revealed that if he set a ticket price of $230 (or today's equivalent of more than $1000) per passenger and sold all the seats on a 707, he could make a profit of $10,000.

While it seemed an attractive financial proposition, Smith was a businessman, and he was wary of becoming involved in the commercial airline industry while knowing so little about it. So his next move was to ask an old friend, journalist Peter Spooner, to test the response by announcing the flight in Sydney's weekend *Sun-Herald* in November 1977.

Smith was stunned by the result. By early next morning his switchboard was jammed and within an hour he had enough passengers to more than fill a 120-seat 707. People were even rushing into his stores and placing money on the counter, much to the surprise of staff who hadn't yet been told about the charter.

By midday, with more than 300 bookings, Smith was on the phone to Qantas with a request to replace the 707 with a 747—and asking if he could book another 747 for a second flight. When Qantas agreed, he then asked for a third but they confessed they couldn't fit a third into their normal schedule commitments.

'Before the flights the publicity was phenomenal and there was even a short article in *The New York Times*,' Smith would recall.

The first flight, called 'Dick Smith's Antarctic Antic', took off from Mascot early on the morning of 13 February 1978. As it headed further south, the only things visible from the plane were the unbroken clouds below. Even though he had been warned by polar experts that the whole continent might be covered in cloud, Smith, sitting in the cockpit peering ahead, became increasingly uneasy.

Then, suddenly, the clouds opened, replaced by the vast, spectacularly white vista of the southern continent. At once relaxed, Smith was also in awe of the scene before him. 'All along the coast we could see where the ice shelves had carved massive bergs into the sea. Further inland mountain peaks pierced the icecap. It was another world.'

As the 747 descended to provide an even better view, passengers rotated between the centre seats and the windows. When the French base at Dumont d'Urville came into view, those above watched as a handful of people, surprised at the sudden appearance of the 747, clambered onto the roof of the main building and began waving wildly. The flight's appearance must have been a rare surprise. 'One guy became so excited he stepped back while waving and fell off the roof into the snow!' Smith remembers.

Then it was on to the south magnetic pole, and while polar experts on board delivered a series of lectures on the continent below the plane turned north for home. Within a month, a second flight ventured south, this time taking in the Admiralty Mountains and the Ross Sea, with one subsequent newspaper headline describing it as 'the day trip of a lifetime'.

Meanwhile, interest had been growing across the Tasman, with Air New Zealand also anxious to grasp the opportunities offered by such a unique tourist destination, but restricted by the range limitations of their DC-8 fleet. That changed, however, with the delivery of their larger DC-10s. Within weeks of Smith's first Qantas flights, Air New Zealand aircraft were also heading south.

Then, in November 1979, disaster struck. Captain Jim Collins' Air New Zealand Flight 901 slammed into Mount Erebus in a white-out. All 237 passengers and the crew of twenty were killed.

The accident brought New Zealand to a standstill and, even more than 40 years on, it is difficult to comprehend its impact on a country with a population of only three million. As one radio commentator pointed out, 'Almost everyone in this country seems connected to the disaster. Although the airline immediately halted all flights, the ramifications of the accident didn't stop there. The agony was further extended by the findings of a royal commission, which revealed evidence of a post-accident cover-up: Air New Zealand had allegedly blamed pilot error when in fact the wrong flight plan had been entered into the aircraft's inertial navigation system. Instead of Collins' DC-10 heading down McMurdo Sound, well to the west of Erebus, the errant flight plan had headed it straight for the almost 8000-metre mountain.

Within months of the accident, Qantas too would halt any further flights. By then, Smith had organised nine 747s to Antarctica, with their festive atmosphere playing host to birthdays and—and in at least two instances—weddings, over the Antarctic ice. His flights also raised almost $100,000 for charities, and supported organisations including NSW National Parks and Wildlife and the Australian Museum.

A further fifteen years would pass before Sydney tour operator Phil Asker sought out Qantas captains Wayne Kearns and Trevor Jensen to ask whether the airline would once again consider operating a Boeing 747 over the Antarctic ice. Jensen had been part of the crew on two earlier flights during the 1970s, but he would soon discover that Erebus had left its mark. Instead of simply lodging a relatively straightforward flight plan down to the Antarctic and back, now there was a requirement to review all previous operational procedures to ensure safety and minimise risk, and a sharper focus on the availability of search-and-rescue facilities if anything went wrong. A much closer involvement by Australia's Antarctic Division itself was also mandated. Qantas needed to comply with changes that applied to all human activities in Antarctica, including a requirement for the airline to provide an environmental impact statement. If such a statement revealed any negative impacts, subsequent evaluation might take up to twelve months.

But the aircraft engine noise and exhaust emissions passed the test. Revised conditions meant that, in contrast to the original flights of the seventies, the 747s would no longer make the low passes over scenic highlights and were instead required to operate at around 10,000 feet. Advance notice would be issued to all parties to the Antarctic Treaty—Australia, New Zealand, the US, Italy and France—so there would be no surprises for the folks at Dumont d'Urville. Qantas captain Alan Terrell, who had been on Antarctic flights, was heard to comment: 'I guess at least now we won't expect anyone to fall off a roof!'

The first Croydon Travel flight took place on New Year's Eve 1994, and the schedule rapidly increased to ten a year, much to the delight of Asker and his team. As the flights continued to attract full loads, Asker was even tempted to plan another from New Zealand but limited interest showed the memories of Erebus were still raw. Not to be discouraged, Asker instead took the courageous step of inviting captain Jim Collins' wife Maria and their four daughters on a flight early in 2013. While Maria Collins declined, three of her daughters accepted. 'It was obviously a very emotional experience for them but they told me it helped them close a chapter,' says Asker. Collins' daughters presented Asker with a copy of *Daughters of Erebus*, the story of the Collins family after the tragedy, written by New Zealand broadcaster Paul Holmes.

As for Qantas and Asker's Antarctica flights: they're still flying, although the days of using 747s have passed into history.

Dick Smith's own innovative use of the 747 didn't stop with the Antarctic. He continued to hire them for flights across Australia's landscape for a variety of other charitable purposes, including one flight in late 1980 when all the passengers, along with the Qantas flight crew, were surnamed Smith. Logically, as Smith explains, 'We used it to raise money for the Smith Family!' Still other 747 charters would be used to support the Pathfinders, a charity organised by Qantas's former and current cabin crew, pilots and ground staff. Since its foundation in 1967 it has raised more than $8 million for charity.

The sheer size and operational flexibility of the 747 also brought advantages beyond charitable causes, one of which was the commemorative occasion often referred to as 'the birth of our nation'—Gallipoli.

24
THE RETURN
OF THE DIGGERS

Aeroplanes can become intrinsically linked to the emotional memories of the people who fly in them. Think of the Darwinians walking across a debris-strewn airport towards their 747 after Cyclone Tracy in 1974, or the Australians leaving a dangerous Beijing after Tiananmen Square in 1989. Yet for the 60 World War I diggers boarding a Qantas aircraft at Mascot in April 1990, it was not a case of 'getting out' but 'going back'—back to a Turkish beach and a battlefield where, three-quarters of a century earlier, they had created a legend.

And while it was once again a government that was organising their travel arrangements to Gallipoli, just as it had been in those early days of World War I, this time it wasn't aboard a troopship but a Boeing 747 specially renamed *Spirit of Anzac* to mark the occasion. And, in further contrast, it's likely that only a small number of those 60 Gallipoli veterans had ever been on a 747 before.

It had taken months of planning by the Department of Veterans' Affairs to reach that day at Mascot. Ensuring it all came together on the Anzac Day of the 75th anniversary involved the complex logistics of transporting a group of men, aged between 90 and 103, in safety and comfort to the other side of the world and back. Much thought, patience and innovation had gone into equipping the *Spirit of Anzac* to ensure the veterans wanted for nothing in the way of medical support and comfort. Twenty-six doctors and nurses, as well as individual carers and an army detachment, were there to accompany them and cater for their every need.

As for the 747 itself: days had been spent converting its first-class section into a fully equipped intensive care unit, with a curtained stretcher area, oxygen cylinders and an array of other medical equipment. The Qantas crew were all volunteers, led by the aircraft's captain Les Hayward, whose father had taken part in the Gallipoli campaign, and cabin crew flight service director Sigmund 'Ziggy' Jablonski, a Vietnam veteran. And just to add to the Qantas connection, two of the Anzac veterans on board, Ernie Guest and Jack Hales, were former Qantas engineers.

Due to the veterans' age, much attention had been paid to making the normal requirements of an international flight as easy as possible, even down to the matter of the standard boarding stairs. At the Qantas hangar at Mascot Jet Base, and on the first stopover, Singapore, a scissor-lift that was normally used for loading cargo transported them directly to the passenger deck.

It wasn't long before the veterans' larrikin streak, which had helped them survive the 'war to end all wars', became evident. Even amid the pomp and ceremony tailored to make this a truly memorable occasion, it was the men themselves who demonstrated they were anything but normal passengers.

One of the earliest signs appeared on their first stopover in Singapore, when one of the diggers failed to turn up for the pre-dinner drinks at their hotel. Organisers immediately feared their worst nightmare had come to pass—and before they had even reached Turkey. After frantic knocks on his door without a response, hotel management arrived with the duplicate key, only to find the digger stretched out, fully clothed and flat on his back on his bed, the door of his room's now-empty bar fridge still open. Much relieved, his carers tucked him in and left him to it.

It wasn't the only incident involving a hotel minibar. One of the main tasks of the mission's small Australian army detachment was to handle the veterans' luggage, but when the time came for departure one of the soldiers expressed surprise at the weight of his veteran's bags. The reason became clear when the bag was opened at Istanbul to reveal the entire contents of a Singapore hotel-room minibar, along with a few monogrammed hotel ashtrays.

As the *Spirit of Anzac* came to a stop at Istanbul airport, and television crews and photographers jostled for position, one of the journey's more memorable yet entirely unscripted moments occurred. Stepping onto Turkish soil for the second time, diminutive, wiry Jack Ryan grasped the hand of the

Turkish Gallipoli veteran there to meet them, greeting him with a piece of long-lost Aussie vernacular: 'It's great to be back—as a cobber!'

It was a much more sombre occasion several days later when, on 25 April, with Australian navy support vessels standing offshore, the sound of the dawn service bugle echoed across the Dardanelles after three-quarters of a century. Then, later that morning, for the diggers it was once again up that brutal escarpment to Lone Pine, this time to hear prime minister Bob Hawke deliver a moving speech and watch an Australian army honour guard march off to the strains of 'Lili Marlene', all beamed back live to Australia by a team from the ABC.

Even for Australia's national broadcaster, the Gallipoli visit was a challenging logistical exercise. Transmitting multiple satellite feeds from broadcast vans on an Anzac beach with no electricity more than 1000 kilometres to Istanbul, to then be relayed to Australia, was no mean feat. Thirty years on, ABC producer Derek Pola describes Gallipoli as 'beautiful, mystical and yet peaceful'. One of his even more vivid memories is hearing one of the veterans insist that members of the accompanying military carry him up the cliffs, this time on a stretcher, so he could revisit the Nek.

When it was over, and still without any 'casualties'—much to the relief of the organisers—the veterans returned to Istanbul to begin their journey home again. Even the boarding process at Istanbul airport next morning delivered its notable moments. Seeing one of the veterans arriving at the door of the

747 with a bandage around his head, a Qantas crew member asked him how he was feeling. 'I'm okay,' he replied. 'I had a bandage around my head the last time I left here too.'

While the guns at Gallipoli might have been silent on that visit, this was not the case a decade later when a Qantas 747 was consigned to another uplift of Aussie diggers—this time into a peacekeeping role in Somalia as part of Operation Solace.

25
THE SOUND OF GUNFIRE IN MOGADISHU

When it comes to Australia's—and for that matter, Qantas's—involvement in the world's conflicts, Somalia barely rates a mention. Wedged between Ethiopia, Djibouti and Kenya to the west, and the Indian Ocean to the east, Somalia achieved independence from Britain and Italy in the 1960s, but its capital Mogadishu was then ravaged by internal conflicts. Power vacuums in the country have, at times, resulted in the breakdown of civilian rule and devastating famine.

Australia's involvement in peacekeeping efforts came after the overthrow of Somalia's then president Siad Barre in early 1991. The outbreak of tribal conflicts led to the creation of Operation Solace, the Australian Defence Force's main contribution to a United Nations–sanctioned multinational peacekeeping force. As a result, in 1993 the task of lifting troops of the 1st Battalion, Royal Australian Regiment, into Mogadishu would fall to Qantas.

It was the first operational deployment of an Australian battalion group since the Vietnam War. For Qantas, too, the operation was reminiscent of the airline's own commitment to flying troops into and out of Vietnam in the 1960s and '70s. Unlike the publicity surrounding Vietnam, however, in the case of Somalia the airline's involvement hardly received a mention in government media announcements at the time.

Some would put this down to a degree of sensitivity within the RAAF to the defence department's choice of aircraft: a Qantas 747 for the troop flights, instead of the RAAF's C-130 Hercules transports. Primarily it was a decision based on the long stage lengths of the two flight sectors required: six hours from Townsville to Singapore, then a further eight from there to Mogadishu, hardly a comfortable journey in cramped C-130s for soldiers expected to deploy the moment they arrived.

For captain Trevor Jensen and those tasked with organising them, the uplifts presented unique logistical challenges. Not least of these were the operational restrictions of Mogadishu itself, with its airport incapable of handling more than one wide-bodied aircraft at a time, and with the emergency restrictions at the airport limiting arrivals and departures to one hour a day. 'Such a nominated window didn't present us with much of a problem as that meant we just had to schedule our departure from Singapore to meet our arrival slot,' recalls Jensen. But Mogadishu's other shortcomings, including a lack of any ground-handling equipment for unloading, no fuel for refuelling and no engineering support, also had to be overcome.

Then there was the vexed question of communications. With none available at Mogadishu to provide an update of weather forecasts and flight plans, it was agreed that Jensen could take the Qantas safety department's satellite phone, which the company had purchased several years earlier for use in any serious accident or incident in an inhospitable area.

These days, Jensen chuckles quietly as he describes the apparatus as a far cry from today's iPhone technology: its handpiece came with a satellite dish that had to be carefully aligned to get a result. Jensen's doubts were not eased when the team decided to test the apparatus several days before they were due to leave, only to discover it didn't work. The company had failed to renew its subscription to Inmarsat, the British global satellite service used for phone and data transmission. 'With that fixed and after watching the fiddling required to set up its aerial I decided to take one of our IT experts with us and in the end they got it to work perfectly,' says Jensen.

Most of the 1st Battalion's support equipment would make its own way to Somalia via the navy vessels HMAS *Tobruk* and *Jervis Bay*, enabling the troops on the 747s to travel light. Their weapons, however, were placed in the 747's hold, in part due to strict regulations on any military personnel transiting Singapore. Even the troops themselves were required to change into civilian clothes before entering Singapore's terminal while the aircraft was being refuelled.

Jensen's team also expected to face another complex set of communications arrangements at the last stage of their journey. A radio link would need to be used from a US Air

Force AWAC aircraft to the aircraft carrier USS *Kittyhawk*, then finally connecting to a controller operating out of the back of a jeep on Mogadishu's airport itself. 'Added to that were USAF F-4 Phantoms, C-130 Hercules and helicopters littering the skies in every direction, having us do a fair bit of ducking and weaving on the final approach,' says flight engineer Norm King.

There to meet them once on the ground was Australia's ground commander Lieutenant Colonel David Hurley, now Australia's governor-general, but with the sound of gunfire in the distance there would be little time for ceremony and it didn't take the anxious troops long to retrieve their weapons from the cargo compartment. One later mission report questioned that particular requirement: 'How could this be when you're alighting from an Australian-owned aircraft with a kangaroo on the tail and your weapons are still in the hold!'

Flight engineer Norm King soon would agree as, with pre-flight checks complete and doors closed, he watched those in the terminal wave goodbye as the 747 began to move away. 'Then suddenly their waves were accompanied by the sound of gunfire and they all dropped to the ground or ducked behind something solid,' he recalls. 'We taxied away at high speed, lined up on the runway and, using maximum take-off thrust, left Mogadishu behind us.' Although King made a precautionary entry in the aircraft's technical log to inspect the Boeing for bullet holes on landing, none were found.

Even heading home came with its own challenges, largely related to fuel. The lack of fuel at Mogadishu meant the 747 had been required to leave Singapore with enough to continue on to the airport in the Seychelles, which, being on an island, required the aircraft to carry two hours of reserve fuel instead of the normal 30 minutes. And just to complicate their Seychelles flight plan, thanks to a coup attempt by mercenaries to take over the government in 1982, the Seychelles airport runway was blocked at sunset every afternoon.

Fortunately the Seychelles requirement wasn't used and, once back in Townsville, Jensen's team then flew the remainder of the battalion to Singapore where another volunteer crew under captain Ken Devenish completed the second Mogadishu mission.

As for the satellite phone? 'We returned it to Ken Lewis in the safety department where it continued to collect dust, and although the subscription was now paid it was never used in an emergency situation,' says Jensen.

The 1st Battalion acted as escorts for more than 400 convoys during their five-month deployment to Somalia, delivering over 8000 tonnes of grain to famine- and drought-stricken villages. Their efforts resulted in the award of two Distinguished Service Crosses, a Distinguished Service Medal, eighteen commendations and one US Legion of Merit.

26

THE 'OSHKOSH
EXPRESS'

Rescuing Australians in times of crisis, taking passengers on sightseeing tours to the Antarctic and flying World War I veterans back to Gallipoli certainly enhanced the 747's reputation with the Australian public. But there remains another lesser-known task that proves beyond doubt the versatility of Joe Sutter's aviation masterpiece.

While most Australians would never have heard of Oshkosh, the ninth-largest city in the US state of Wisconsin, its annual air show attracts thousands of the world's aviation enthusiasts. Wisconsin might also be a long way from any of Qantas's regular air routes but in the 1980s it figured in one of the airline's most unusual charter operations: in 1981, a Qantas 747 Combi achieved a record by carrying the most pilots ever—292—in one aircraft. And that wasn't all: packed behind them on the aircraft's main deck as cargo were *twelve* Australian-built light aircraft to take part in the show.

The appearance of a Qantas 747 in such an unusual setting began as a 'thought bubble' by Qantas flight engineer Dave Thomas on his first visit to Oshkosh in 1980. A sports aviation enthusiast in his spare time, and a member of Sport Aircraft Association of Australia (SAAA), Thomas was standing with Qantas captain Bob Rosewarne when they heard over the public address system that unfortunately one of the show's popular aerobatic pilots, Jim Lacy, wouldn't be performing. 'But if everyone would like to look to the south . . .', the announcement continued—and with that Thomas watched as a United Airlines DC-8 appeared, flown by captain Jim Lacy in his normal role as an airline pilot, and executed a series of flypasts.

'Wouldn't it be something if that was a Red Tail doing that?' asked Thomas. Rosewarne too could see the value.

Once back in Sydney, Rosewarne bounced the idea around with director of flight operations Alan Terrell, who immediately saw the benefits of Qantas being part of one of the world's best known air shows. 'Without Terrell there would never have been an Oshkosh Express,' says Thomas. He then set out to test the interest by placing an advertisement in the Sport Aircraft Association's magazine. The response was overwhelming. When a similar reaction came from the US's Experimental Aircraft Association, the air show's organisers, the Qantas team began a feasibility study of the logistics of getting aboard not only a bunch of enthusiasts but some of their aircraft as well. Another of Thomas's flight engineer colleagues, Keith Gordon, joined the team, and they set out to see if it would be possible.

The first obvious problem was the length of Oshkosh's runway, which was far too short to handle a 747. So they began to look at whether Chicago's O'Hare, one of the world's busiest airports, would be an option. That idea didn't last long: 'When the O'Hare airport manager heard that a bunch of foreign pilots, with home-built aeroplanes, might want to put them together on his ramp and then taxi out to join a line of departing jets he had a fit, so there was no way that was going to work,' says Thomas.

So it was Milwaukee, about 135 kilometres away, that was the only option for the Qantas 747. There the dozen aircraft on board would be assembled and flown on to Oshkosh, while buses took the remainder of the passengers destined for the air show. Then, for Thomas and his team, came an even more historic achievement when the Australian War Memorial agreed to allow their replica of Qantas's first aircraft, the Avro 504K, to be flown to San Francisco where it would be reassembled and trucked overland to Oshkosh in time for the air show.

Gordon remembers well the excitement among the thousands at Oshkosh when, with Qantas's director of line operations Ken Davenport at the controls, the Qantas Combi opened the show with a low-level flypast at around 300 feet above the Oshkosh runway. While most of the crowd might have savoured the moment, unfortunately for Davenport an Australian Civil Aviation Authority (CAA) official among them was less impressed. Davenport himself would always argue he had approval for 300 feet, but the CAA maintained it had only approved a flypast at 500 feet, with the result that back at Qantas at Mascot he was demoted to 'flying a desk' for six months.

Whatever the rights or wrongs of that flypast, the appearance of the Qantas 747 at the air show would have long-term implications for Oshkosh itself. When Dave Thomas arrived at Oshkosh the following year, the organisers told him they wanted to do it all again. Thomas cautioned them: 'We can't land here because the runway is too short for a 747 and it gets to be too expensive to bus the people up from Milwaukee.'

'Then leave it with us,' came the response.

Thomas is convinced he was therefore at least partly responsible for the EAA extending the length of Oshkosh's north–south runway to take a 747. 'When I took the second Oshkosh Express flight to Oshkosh in 1989 we were the first international wide-bodied aircraft full of people to land there.'

By that time Thomas had formed his own company, Avtours, which would ultimately arrange four annual Oshkosh visits up to 1998—although the original 1981 visit would be the only occasion when the Australians took their own aircraft with them. And thanks to a little 'creative accounting', it hadn't cost them much: 'We didn't charge them for their aircraft. They went along as "luggage" both ways!'

But while much publicity would accompany 747 charters to such destinations as the Antarctic, Gallipoli and Oshkosh, other charters of a Qantas 747 would take place much more quietly behind the closed doors of national security. At least one had the primary aim of countering airborne terrorism.

27
'THIS 747 IS A WHOLE NEW BALL GAME'

It's a comment about the 747 that could be expected to come from a wide range of people, from pilots and cabin crew, to ground engineers, refuellers and cargo handlers—in fact, anyone who learned to deal with this new giant of the skies. But it's actually attributed to another organisation normally operating well outside the commercial aviation industry, whose association with the 747 usually remained well hidden from the public gaze.

Australia's Special Air Service (SAS) Regiment generally operated 'under the radar' as far as the general public was concerned, ever since its earliest days of reconnaissance behind the lines in Borneo during the Indonesian Konfrontasi of the 1960s, and later in the Vietnam War. Part of its success relied on its whereabouts being unknown by the enemy, and often the regiment would be in situ in conflict zones long before their presence was publicly announced. Much of that changed in later years when successive Australian governments appeared with them at their home base at Swanbourne in Perth. While it might have been a useful publicity opportunity for government ministers to 'farewell' the unit prior to its departure for a war, such occasions were often regarded by those associated with the unit as of doubtful advantage to their operations.

When it came to acts of terrorism and aircraft hijackings, however, particularly during the late 1960s and '70s, the exposure to the public of such special forces could hardly be avoided. These were the days of the Boeing 707 and the DC-8, large in comparison to their propeller-driven predecessors, but both still less than half the size of the Boeing 747.

In Australia, the only 747s available for SAS training belonged to Qantas, and over many years the two organisations formed a close relationship while preparing for an event both parties hope will never occur. To meet this training requirement, Qantas developed its own security and operations team comprising pilots, flight engineers and cabin crew, who filled the essential company roles to allow the SAS to develop their skills. The primary aim of the SAS was to achieve sufficient surprise to dominate the aircraft within minutes, preventing hijackers from having any opportunity to turn their guns on their hostages or detonate explosives—in other words, overcoming hijackers with minimum casualties.

With the 747, such exercises would be held annually whenever possible, although much of the timing depended on when a jumbo could be released from its regular Qantas scheduling commitments to meet the type of training the SAS required. For instance, a ground-assault exercise might require an aircraft to be parked for several days on a remote site at an airport while the SAS and state police special operations units went about the business of refining their tactics, not only on the ground but occasionally in the air as well.

Qantas cabin crew safety manager Bob Parker was there in the early 1970s when the SAS first began to hone its skills on an aircraft twice the size of any they'd ever had to work with before. On that first occasion, the site chosen was the RAAF base at Amberley in Queensland, with the 747 positioned there overnight by Qantas captain Geoff Molloy and his small hijack security team.

Parker watched next morning as the 50 soldiers who would act as 'passengers' for the exercise arrived. 'It appeared they all thought they were in for a nice day sitting around in a 747 so there was a bit of disappointment when the beer and refreshments they'd brought along for the occasion were immediately confiscated and they were told, "Just sit there and do nothing."' Parker and his team were told to do the same.

They were still sitting there several hours later when suddenly the doors flew open and black-clad, masked SAS troops started screaming at those on board to stay in their seats and to put their hands on their heads.

'It was bloody frightening,' says Parker, who soon learned how serious they were when he briefly rose in his seat in an attempt to see what was happening further up in the aircraft— only to have the SAS trooper standing nearby hit him over the ear and shout at him to sit down. 'They were strategically standing in doorways and you could see they had the whole aeroplane covered and in position to be able to shoot anyone who attempted to move,' he recalls.

Parker says it became obvious, even before they boarded, that the SAS knew who the Qantas crew members were. Within seconds, Parker's wrists were tied and he was frogmarched along the aisle to one of the aircraft's front doors, where a ladder led to the ground. When he reached the bottom of the ladder he found Geoff Molloy and the rest of the crew lying facedown on the tarmac. 'Then when everyone was identified, the ties were cut off and it was all over.'

While the Qantas teams always realised that something dramatic was bound to happen in SAS training, the surprise often came from an unexpected direction. On another hijack exercise, this time in the air between Sydney and Melbourne, it soon became obvious that several of the army passengers in civilian clothes had been planted there as hijackers. One of them, near Parker, suddenly leapt from his seat and put a gun to Parker's head.

After landing at Tullamarine, the aircraft was remotely parked and the exercise continued throughout the day. Parker insists no one from Qantas who took part was ever in any doubt about the authenticity of the exercises. 'Everyone's watches would be taken off them, the flight crew would be pulled out of the cockpit, their badges of rank ripped off them as they were placed under guard.'

On one occasion the chief hijacker took the whole crew

up to the lounge in the 747 and subjected them to a twenty-minute harangue as to why he was taking over the plane. 'He would have got an Oscar for the acting, as he alternated from talking in a normal voice to bursts of screaming and shouting. It was quite frightening, actually. On other exercises several of the hijackers would take up normal seats among the passengers and the assault team would have to identify them from the rest.'

Parker says that, in contrast to the Boeing 707 days, the sheer size of the 747 presented much bigger problems when it came to handling such crises as bomb scares. Even back on those 707 days, when Bill Selwyn and his crew faced 'The Mr Brown Affair', searching all the nooks and crannies where a device might be hidden took up vital hours. But the sheer size of the 747 and the time required to search the aircraft led to the airline developing its own specific bomb scare document. Kept under lock and key on the flight deck, it identified even the smallest opening on the aircraft. 'Thanks to that,' says Parker, 'we were able to rapidly locate something the size of a tissue box!'

Despite the often long and intense hours of such exercises, Parker says there was never any shortage of cabin crew volunteers to take part. 'We in fact tried to spread it around the crews as much as possible in the hope that if something serious ever did occur there might be at least one of them on board who had been through such an exercise.'

While Parker witnessed what went on from the passenger viewpoint, former SAS member Kerry Danes, an assault commander on one of the teams assigned to 'recover a 747', saw it from the other side. 'The aim was to saturate, secure and dominate the aircraft in the shortest possible time to ensure the terrorists had limited time to react,' says Danes. 'From the time we were told to execute we would have cleared all the areas we were responsible for within ten seconds.' Danes says such exercises were essential to maintain what was universally regarded 'as the regiment's world-class aircraft assault capability'.

Over the years, many in Qantas developed a close relationship with the SAS and would occasionally be invited to watch them honing their skills at the regiment's base at Swanbourne, particularly in what was known as the regiment's 'killing house', a room specially designed for hostage rescue training. On such occasions several of the Qantas people would be directed to sit in a lounge chair in the middle of the room, before an SAS trooper turned out the lights, with a warning: 'Whatever you hear or see, don't dare move!'

A few quiet minutes would pass before they were startled by the sound of a door crashing open, immediately followed by a series of shots ringing out as narrow beams of light split the darkness. Then, finally, there would be a brief flash of light as dark figures exited by an opposite doorway. When the lights came on the Qantas pair would look behind them to see that, unnoticed by them, several wooden, man-sized 'hostage' images had been placed behind their lounge chairs, both now bearing bullet wounds to their heads.

Like Bob Parker, flight operations safety chief Ken Lewis found such visits to be among the highlights of a long Qantas career. 'I found the SAS guys amongst the nicest and most professional I ever worked with.'

28
REARRANGING THE DECKCHAIRS

For the average airline passenger, all that matters when they look at their airline ticket are the city names for the origin and destination and the dates and times of their flights. Beyond that, a ticket gives no indication of the negotiations that have taken place between various governments and their designated carriers to ensure this complex international airline system actually works. But if you asked any senior airline marketing executive of the 747 era which word would haunt them most, the answer would invariably be 'overcapacity'.

By the time the Boeing 747 arrived on the scene in the early 1970s, many factors were forcing airlines like Qantas to tackle the task of filling literally hundreds of seats while competing with an increasing number of Asian airlines, many with staff cost structures well below the Australian level, all vying to attract the same passenger. Former Qantas chief executive John Ward puts it this way:

These aggressively competitive airlines presented a challenge to the established international regulatory framework which had for many years been enshrined through the system of bilateral treaties known as air services agreements, themselves governed by multinational conventions.

By virtue of geography and their lower labour costs, they were able to offer attractive products which quickly began to erode the Australia–Europe market which up until now had been the mainstay of Qantas profitability.

Thus while, historically, overcoming the tyranny of distance had spurred Qantas international expansion and defined the airline's character as an end-of-the-line carrier, its geographical location had left it with little control over its own destiny in its traditional end-to-end European market.

So the airline created 'The Red Book', developed by Ward and his policy group under the direction of chief executive Keith Hamilton and presented to the Australian government in early 1978. Its benign title barely suggested its groundbreaking aim: to convince the government to renegotiate air services agreements and limit the Australian market to those airlines with treaty access to 'traffic'—airline negotiating parlance for the passenger.

The result was Australia's International Civil Aviation Policy, or ICAP, which restricted intermediate carriers like Singapore Airlines and Malaysian Airlines to carrying only 'genuine' passenger traffic between Australia and Singapore or Australia and Malaysia. ICAP effectively cut out the Asian airlines' access to the direct Australia, UK and Europe market.

Within a changing, intensely competitive international airline environment, it didn't take long for ICAP to become the target of a relentless campaign by the Asian airlines against 'Australian protectionism', a campaign that doomed ICAP to failure within three years. Coupled with a US-led move towards 'open skies' with its designation of multiple 'national' carriers, an additional thrust came from yet another direction: charter flights from the UK and Europe.

Once again, at least as far as charters were concerned, it was a question of raw economics. Put in the simplest terms, the charter concept meant that while a national carrier was required to operate a scheduled service on a set day at a set time, even if it was half empty and therefore operating below cost, the charter operator could offer a fare cheap enough to attract a full aeroplane but still high enough to make the flight pay for itself.

Also of major concern to Qantas was a British decision to allow unregulated charter flights between South-East Asia and Europe, using Singapore and Kuala Lumpur as ports at which passengers heading for Europe could join a cheaper British charter flight.

This dual dilemma forced Qantas to be become increasingly creative. Soon it came up with the concept of using a location in Asia to develop a 'hub and spoke' pattern of services, which would more efficiently link Australia's widely spaced centres of population with Europe and London and even other parts of Asia. In most respects, Singapore would become the key.

Take the Kangaroo Route to the UK, for instance. While there might not be enough end-to-end traffic to justify a service operated solely between any specific Australian capital city such as Perth or Adelaide, by coordinating flight timings to arrive within an hour of each other at Singapore's extremely efficient Changi airport, passengers could join the traditional through-flights out of Sydney to London or points in Europe. On the return journey to Australia, the same Singapore hub-and-spoke concept was simply used in reverse, with passengers transferring to their Perth or Adelaide destination while their original flight from London continued on to Sydney.

Although parts of the original concept dated back to the 707 days, its application now in the 1970s made even more sense when utilising the improved operating costs of the Boeing 747—and the need to fill it.

Along with such innovations in scheduling came the introduction of lower fares for long-haul travel to ports in the UK or Europe which, although based on carefully restricted conditions, were attractive enough to enable the airline to attract passengers away from the charter operators. 'The task was to develop a pricing, marketing and capacity-management agenda which would underpin our entry into an era of profitable and affordable mass travel,' Ward explains.

The results came in the form of a Sydney-to-London $700 return fare (more than $7000 in today's currency) alongside a $420 one-way fare, which opened up a whole range of new market segments to Australian travellers. Not only did such fares deliver the opportunity for cheap long-haul vocational travel, but offered a 'visiting friends and relatives' (VFR) opportunity that attracted thousands of migrants who had settled in Australia after World War II. As Ward notes, 'In addition to making money for us, for many of those going to visit former homelands in Europe for such a price it had significant social and cultural aspects.'

The explosion in demand that followed was nothing short of extraordinary, with Australia–UK traffic growing by 50 per cent in 1973–74 alone. Not that the pragmatic Singaporeans missed out on trading such rights to their own advantage, in return achieving additional weekly flights to access an Australian passenger market many times larger and more lucrative than their own. As for the original ICAP idea—even Keith Hamilton himself would later question its origins, once admitting that his airline 'went willingly or otherwise down the wrong road'.

And while the pricing regime developed under Ward and his team meant that Qantas was now finally able to overcome its geographical disadvantage and thus control its end-to-end Australia–Europe market, the airline's London-based Ken Groves saw the impact of such fares from the far end of the route. He watched as his airline added Manchester in the north of England to cater for the valuable VFR market.

Groves also credits an earlier fare initiative, the Pacesetter, as offering a more attractive alternative to a month-long journey to London aboard vessels such as the *Fairstar*, which had for decades served as a rite of passage for many younger

Australians on their first journey to the UK. Once the 747 was introduced, other marketing strategies began to benefit from the fare flexibility it offered.

***

Event sponsorship had long been a staple of the jet age. In the 707 era, sponsorship often centred around what many at Qantas called 'the board director's wife syndrome', favouring particular charities or cultural pursuits. Indeed, the airline had its own art gallery in London for regular exhibitions by the likes of Sidney Nolan and other internationally known Australian artists. Although such ventures were not designed to attract passengers, having its own recognised gallery in London did bring the airline one considerable side benefit: in some instances, it accepted valuable pieces of the art on show as part-payment for shipping them to London, which over time resulted in Qantas acquiring a valuable art collection of its own.

But it wasn't long before the business of event sponsorship began to move beyond the art world. By the mid-1980s, local entrepreneurs were enticing New Zealanders across the Tasman on $600 weekend packages to Melbourne and Sydney for stage shows such as *Cats*, *Les Misérables* and *The Phantom of the Opera*. 'We also made millions out of *Buddy* and *Miss Saigon* over the next ten years,' says Groves, although along with all the glitter and high excitement of showbiz sponsorship would come the unpredictability and anxiety of dealing with stars.

Elton John's 1986 concert tour, called Tour de Force, broke new ground for Qantas as it began to move away from its traditionally conservative promotional image. It was the first time Elton John had performed with a complete symphony orchestra. With concerts scheduled in Melbourne, Adelaide, Perth, Brisbane and Sydney, the tour brought an assortment of logistical challenges. Along with transporting musicians and their instruments, Qantas had to manage Elton John's requirement for around 50 sound and other technicians, plus the star's own tonne of baggage, at times requiring the airline's ground controllers to turn a blind eye to some of the load requirements.

Then, in the middle of it all, in Perth, Elton John lost his voice, forcing him to cancel a show and for a time placing the coming Sydney schedule at risk until Groves' group managed to negotiate new arrangements to get the bulkier equipment back to the east coast.

For Groves, Sydney would have its moments, particularly when he talked Elton John into agreeing to open a new Qantas office. Unfortunately for Groves, when the star arrived at the site he realised it wasn't the opening of a new multistorey Qantas building but a small street-front sales office. 'Given he was all dressed up for it he was pretty bloody annoyed,' Groves recalls.

For Qantas, the Elton John extravaganza would soon be matched by such shows as *The Three Tenors*, and tours by Diana Ross and other international artists. Despite a few missteps, Groves says Qantas's market dominance and the capacity of the 747 established the airline as the brand leader in the entertainment field.

29
SAVING OUR
'QUEEN OF THE SKIES'

Aviation people have a sentimental quirk when it comes to parting company with particular aeroplanes. They often just don't want to say goodbye.

Most often, this is a way of paying tribute to a particular machine's role in a generation of flight, whether it be Britain's famous Spitfire of World War II or, in Australia's case, Smithy and Ulm's *Southern Cross*, which contributed so much towards establishing Australia's unique aviation heritage. Some, like the DC-3, born out of the wartime C-47, have become part of commercial folklore mainly due to the part they played in transitioning aviation from war to peacetime.

In Australia, because of its geographical isolation and the tyranny of distance between its far-flung shorelines, particular aircraft have embedded themselves in the psyche of many Australians who would normally have only a passing interest in aviation. Take, for instance, the easily recognisable shape of the Lockheed Constellation with which Qantas first circled the globe, or the memorable Boeing 707, on the wings of which it entered the jet age.

But while that same jet age would slash flight times in half and open the world to affordable travel, efficiency and design requirements began to blur the noticeable differences between the airliners themselves. To the average traveller, for instance, the DC-8 looked much like the 707, while the DC-10 partly matched the style of Lockheed's L-1011.

The Boeing 747, however, would change all that. It created its own identity in Australia to such an extent that by the time of its inevitable retirement from Qantas service, steps would be taken to make sure some of those Qantas 747s would be saved. After writing their own chapter in Australian's history over more than 50 years, these aircraft would not all go the same way as thousands of others—either resold, or ending their days in airport graveyards in California or Arizona. Two would remain on Australian soil to be enjoyed by thousands of Australians.

It was thanks to the generosity, passion and foresight of a dedicated group in Qantas, and the enthusiasm of two of Australia's primary aviation museums—the Qantas Founders Museum in Longreach, Queensland, and the Historical Aircraft Restoration Society (HARS) Aviation Museum at Albion Park, south of Wollongong—that these two aircraft were saved. The gifting of the 747s to these two museums took place thirteen years apart, and demonstrated the depth of the emotional link and deep respect between people and particular machines.

***

The original idea of a Boeing 747 for Longreach came in early 2001 with the approaching retirement of some of the airline's earliest 747-200s. While previously, former Qantas Boeings had been renowned for commanding a premium price on the second-hand aircraft market, those days had passed. Now their inevitable fate was being broken up in an American desert.

A meeting of minds between Qantas's then head of aircraft operations David Forsyth and his close colleague, senior production engineer Bob Sprague, gave shape to the idea. 'Since both of us were board members of the Longreach museum it didn't take us long to come up with the idea of perhaps donating one,' recalls Forsyth. He then took the proposal to the airline's board. If board approval could be achieved, it would then be up to Sprague to make it happen.

'Donating an aircraft—and a bloody big one at that—was a first for Qantas and the first question I had to ask the aircraft performance group was whether a 747 could even land at Longreach,' says Sprague. 'When they did their calculations and said it was possible—with some reservations—I took that as a definite yes, so the project began, to become one of the biggest and most interesting projects I ever had in Qantas. It would involve just about every area in the airline with the exception of ticket sales!'

And the aircraft that was the focus of this exercise? Boeing 747-238 VH-EBQ *City of Bunbury* came with several built-in advantages, not least the 'Q' to match its state destination. The second was its excellent condition: it had the best paint job of all the 747s Sprague and his team had to choose from, a result of a complete repaint two years ago.

Longreach airport itself faced some unusual challenges in preparing for a 747. Not least was the need to devise a ground-anchoring system that would prevent the 747's large tail fin from behaving like a weathervane, and potentially moving the aircraft in a high wind. Thinking Seattle might have the answer, Sprague and his team quickly turned to them for some suggestions, only to learn that Boeing weren't able to help. 'They'd never been asked how to permanently display a 747!' says Sprague. So it fell to a support team under licensed aircraft maintenance engineer Jeff Swinson to learn the basics of how to build formwork, mix concrete, drill holes and glue anchor bolts into place to secure the aircraft.

Meanwhile, Qantas flight operations pilots under the chief of the -200 fleet, captain Mike Fitzgerald, began familiarising themselves with Longreach airport. The process which began with Fitzgerald, who would command the flight, sitting in the cockpit jump seat of a Qantas 737 on a charter flight to Longreach. As an extra measure, he arranged for another Qantas pilot to take a video camera and shoot the approach to Longreach airfield from a local joyflight helicopter to supplement the simulator experience. Then it was back to the airline's flight simulator at Mascot, where part of the narrow taxiway at Avalon aerodrome, near Geelong, was programmed in to replicate Longreach's limitations.

With preparations now underway, it was up to Qantas engineering planning, responsible for 747 schedules, to decide on a release date for *City of Bunbury*. When Sprague requested a date in early November 2002, he was told late November was the only option, which resulted in a surprise coincidence, says Sprague: 'So we compromised on 16 November, without initially realising the significance. It was the company's birthday!'

Saturday, 16 November dawned fine and clear at Longreach and the build-up in expectations had now reached its peak. Local resident Tom Harwood had more of a vested interest in the event than most. Aside from having been closely involved in the museum project for eleven years, he was also the ABC's regional program manager for Western Queensland and would lead the team for the outdoor broadcast of *City of Bunbury*'s arrival. It would be beamed live across the state.

'At that time around 3500 lived in the town but the population at the aerodrome that day was estimated to be closer to 5000. Some businesses in the town didn't even bother to open their doors that morning and the pubs even stayed closed until midday so staff could watch the landing,' Harwood recalls. 'Our Saturday presenter Ross Hall started his program at the Qantas hangar at 6 a.m. but during the next couple of hours our entire station team arrived, without being asked, to assist in any way they could.'

As Mike Fitzgerald flew *City of Bunbury* slowly across the aerodrome and joined the circuit to land, Harwood remembers a 'deathly silence' among the crowd. That changed to cheers and whistles of approval as the wheels touched down and the 747 taxied to the wider portion at the end of the runway.

There, due to the surface width restrictions, it took half an hour for a tug to swing it through a nine-point turn and back towards the waiting crowd.

Even a hardened old reporter like Harwood confessed to shedding a tear when the engines shut down for the last time. 'It was like seeing and hearing a living thing dying but that was really just the end of that phase of life for EBQ. Unlike so many of its scrapped colleagues it was about to undergo preparation for a new life, which continues today.'

And that life has certainly brought a rare opportunity to many. Since 2002, almost half a million visitors to the museum have passed through inspections of *City of Bunbury*, ironically many of them under the guidance of Tom Harwood, who went on to become the museum's curator.

The final word on that day probably belongs to Qantas chair Margaret Jackson at the official welcoming ceremony. 'I'm not sure there are many chairmen in the airline business who have actually given away a 747.' She couldn't have foreseen that in thirteen years' time such a rare gift would happen again with the retirement of an even more memorable 747, VH-OJA, bringing with it similar emotional responses. It, too, would present its own set of operational challenges as it headed for its final resting place—the HARS Aviation Museum at Albion Park.

***

It was late 2014 when the documentation for the sale of VH-OJA *City of Canberra* arrived on the desk of Qantas's chief financial officer Gareth Evans. The buying and selling of aircraft was part of Evans' responsibility, and *City of Canberra* was simply the latest of the 747s to reach the end of its useful life, to be replaced by a range of new Airbus versions across the airline's international fleet.

In contrast to the circumstances under which other 747-400s had left the fleet over the previous year, selling *City of Canberra* to another airline was no longer an option. It seemed as if its final destination would be the Arizona desert, joining the hundreds of other retired jets being sold as scrap. For Evans, however, this one was different: 'When the document arrived I actually sat there with it in front of me, my pen poised over it, and I just couldn't bring myself to sign it. After all, this was an aircraft which had created a distance record on its delivery flight and was part of Australia's aviation history.'

So back went the paperwork and within a matter of weeks Evans' government affairs and fleet trading staff had come up with the HARS solution. As in the case of the Long-reach relocation, the gift to HARS at Albion Park's Illawarra Regional Airport (now Shellharbour Airport), 90 kilometres south of Sydney, brought logistical challenges—the first being a runway only 1819 metres long and 30 metres wide. A detailed engineering process would also be needed, to apply reinforcements to the airport's taxiway, and to install steel and concrete on the permanent hard stand to support the aircraft's stripped-down weight of more than 150 tonnes.

Once that was underway, the airline's flight operations people began putting together the aircraft's delivery plan.

For the air crew who would operate the flight—captains Greg Matthews and Ossie Miller, first officer David Hagley and second officer Michael East—it was back to Mascot's flight simulator to select the route and how to configure the aircraft for landing in the limited time available between take-off and approach to Albion Park airport. Its take-off would be over Botany Bay, then out to sea before crossing the coast just short of Wollongong. To familiarise the crew with the terrain around Albion Park, particularly its proximity to the Great Dividing Range, HARS took them aboard its Lockheed Neptune for a pilot's-eye view of the area.

Sunday, 8 March 2015 was fine and clear as *City of Canberra* taxied through the traditional farewell for an aircraft leaving an airport on its last flight—an arch of water from two fire-fighting tenders. A very lightweight VH-OJA was soon in the air, headed towards the thousands of onlookers who had gathered around Albion Park to watch it touch down shortly before 8 a.m. It was another 747 milestone, to join its non-stop 20 hours, 9 minutes and 5 seconds from London to Sydney fifteen years before: the flight from Mascot had taken a mere eleven minutes, another record for a Boeing 747.

After taxiing to a stop at the end of the runway, a tug towed it to a reception that received worldwide media coverage. Among those there to welcome it were three of the pilots, captains David Massy-Greene, Ray Heiniger and Rob Greenop, who had flown *City of Canberra* into the record books in 1989. Sadly, their colleague captain George Lindeman had passed away.

Since that day, more than 210,000 visitors have passed through *City of Canberra*, one of the south coast's most popular tourist attractions—and, as in the case of Longreach's *City of Bunbury*, a lasting memorial to a bygone era.

30
THE FINAL
FAREWELL

The fateful day finally arrived on 22 July 2020, just weeks short of 50 years since the first Qantas 747 touched down at Mascot. Had it not been for the downturn in travel created by the ravages of COVID-19, the Queen of the Skies might have easily made it to the half-century. In those years, 747s had flown 3.6 billion kilometres in Qantas service, the equivalent of 4700 return trips to the Moon, or 90,000 trips around the world.

In response to requests from its employees and customers to say farewell, Qantas scheduled three one-hour flights in the weeks prior to its departure: one each out of Sydney, Melbourne and Brisbane, with profits donated to the HARS and Longreach museums.

The Boeing VH-OEJ *Wunala* was the final 747 to fly over eastern Australia. It had been seventeen years in Qantas service and although its farewell hardly matched the pomp and ceremony of the arrival of her predecessor *City of Canberra* in 1971, *Wunala's* departure would bring its own emotional signatures. Making comparisons in such cases can difficult but when looked at in terms of a half-century of Qantas history two things come to mind.

Qantas chief executive Alan Joyce, who farewelled *Wunala* at a moving ceremony in its Mascot hangar, was five years old and growing up in Tallaght, Dublin, when the first 747-200 arrived at Qantas in August 1971. Captain Sharelle Quinn, who would command its final flight into the history books, was Qantas's first female captain and had flown the aircraft for 36 years. When the first 747 had arrived in Australia, 50 years before, Qantas had no female pilots at all.

One of the small, sentimental touches to occur during that farewell ceremony was an invitation to those attending to scrawl personal tributes in marker pen on the aircraft's fuselage before it was pushed out of the hangar to fly off into history. Among the more surprising was one that simply said 'A job well done, Joe Sutter,' which prompted one old Qantas hand to later comment, 'It was wonderful to see that at least a few there still had a memory which went back to the man critical to the success of the Boeing dream!'

The pre-departure ceremony at Mascot, and the flypasts across Sydney Harbour and the HARS museum at Albion Park, were also a salute to an airline now celebrating its centenary year and to the many thousands of men and women who had been part of the enterprise and at times drama of the airline's 100 years. As one of them suggested: 'For most of us this aeroplane defined our young and not-so-young days, with the noise of her engines the soundtrack of our working lives.'

In his farewell speech, Joyce acknowledged that the 747 had changed the face of aviation and had put international travel within reach of the average Australian. 'It's hard to overstate the impact it had on aviation and a country as far away as Australia,' he noted.

Beyond the guests in that hangar, other former Qantas staff would pay their own tributes. Standing on Shep's Mound, a grassy knoll just off Sydney's main runway, was flight engineer Norm King, wearing his old Qantas uniform for the first time in eighteen years and holding an Australian flag. 'I thought I was being a bit over the top until I noticed many around me in uniforms representing various Qantas departments, so my embarrassment soon faded!' Meanwhile, waiting on yet another hillside, this time with a view across Albion Park's runway, was former captain Gordon Power and several of his old Qantas colleagues, each with a glass of champagne in hand and ready to drink a toast.

Spectacular flypasts have long been a tradition when celebrating the end of an era in aviation, and this occasion would be no exception as Sharelle Quinn brought *Wunala* across Albion Park at an altitude of 1500 feet. Many would, however, notice that the nature of such farewells had changed since the days of Ken Davenport at Oshkosh's air show, and Alan Terrell introducing the SP to the Queensland coast by providing those on the ground a much closer view of the underneath of the 747 as it crossed over them.

Gordon Power probably summed it up best at Albion Park that afternoon when he raised his glass of champagne towards VH-OEJ as she turned gently north-east for the last time: 'Thanks, old friend. Travel safe.'

After delivering a farewell over the radio to *City of Canberra*, its sister 747 on the ground, Quinn banked away over the Pacific but it didn't take long for plane spotters tracking her course to realise that something was amiss. That parting radio message wasn't to be *Wunala's* final tribute. In fact, *Wunala* was heading north towards Newcastle to once again prove that some in the airline had lost none of their talent for surprise and innovation.

You could say *Wunala's* cockpit was heavily loaded with captains that day. Along with Quinn were three other captains: Ewen Cameron, the airline's longest serving 747 pilot, with more than 40 years on the type; the airline's 747 fleet manager Owen Weaver; and Weaver's fleet deputy, Greg Fitzgerald. What was about to happen had been Weaver's pet project for many months prior to *Wunala's* departure. Quinn was following a flight-path pattern, known as Skyart ROO, that would draw the outline of the airline's famous flying kangaroo in the sky over Australia's east coast.

Such an exercise might appear easy to the outside observer but in reality its achievement relied on a complex set of circumstances, not least the input of around 100 or so 'waypoints' into the aircraft's navigation system, requiring many hours in a flight simulator. Added to that were approvals from both the Civil Aviation Safety Authority and the RAAF base at

Williamstown, as the 'back' and 'tail' parts of the roo would be in air force airspace. Then there was the 747's heavy take-off weight of 385 tonnes, as it would then fly more than thirteen hours to Los Angeles. Such a heavy weight reduced the margins when it came to manoeuvring through the tight turns required.

'The day of departure started early for Owen and I as the . . . waypoints had to be manually entered into the aircraft's flight management computer, a job which took nearly two hours,' recalls Greg Fitzgerald. 'And with the waypoints being so close together we needed to check and double-check them to ensure the Skyart looked like a kangaroo and not a wombat!'

The intense work over many hours paid dividends, however, and the 90-minute flight sequence went off without a hitch, coming up with a radar image in the shape of a kangaroo—even down to its head and paws—which immediately gained attention around the world. It was a befitting end to an icon that had secured a prime place in Australian aviation history.

Two days later, after a water-cannon salute at Los Angeles airport, the last of Qantas's 747s set off on its final twenty minutes of flight to Mojave. Even that last stretch had its complications, says Fitzgerald:

Approaching Mojave airport, with about 8 nautical miles [15 kilometres] to run, a Cessna 172 popped up ahead of us, at our altitude, so we immediately climbed from 5500 to 9000 feet to start the approach again. Just when we thought it was all over! The rest of the approach was uneventful, however, and may I say that the last landing of the last Qantas 747 by Ewen Cameron was as smooth as silk, or as we say in the industry, a greaser—as the Queen deserved.

It would be the last flight in command for Fitzgerald and Cameron before their own retirements, both with more than with 20,000 hours in their logbooks.

The final entry in *Wunala*'s paperwork, in its technical log dated 24 July 2020 and signed by Cameron and Fitzgerald, perhaps says it all:

'FINISHED WITH ENGINES—FOR THE LAST TIME. FAREWELL.'

REFLECTIONS

While *Wunala*'s departure in July 2020 brought down the curtain on the Boeing 747 in Qantas service, it also left behind a historical legacy that is kept alive by former staff, and that has a scope arguably unmatched by any other Australian organisation. Across Australia, and a brace of Qantas ports around the globe, former staff still gather regularly to catch up and reminisce about old times. These former pilots, flight engineers and cabin crew meet regularly and keep in touch via newsletters.

Many of those who worked in engineering or in ground-support roles at Mascot also stay in touch. Still others have taken the opportunity to get up close and personal with the aircraft engines and airframes that formed such a large part of their working lives, the Historical Aircraft Restoration Society (HARS) at Shellharbour Airport being a prime example.

Around 100 of the 700 who maintain HARS aircraft in an airworthy condition are volunteers who have retired after long careers at Qantas. As another of the HARS volunteers puts it: 'Many say they come to obtain their fix of avgas!' They also enjoy the nostalgia of working in close proximity to several icons of Qantas's earlier days—the DC-3 and the Lockheed Super Constellation, the latter recovered from the Arizona desert in the 1990s. 'Connie', as it is known, is now the only Super Constellation in the world still flying, a fact that owes much to the skill of a small group of former engineers known at HARS as the 'Class of '56'—the year they joined Qantas.

Beyond these operational and ground-support groups, there exists a plethora of former staff who meet regularly, among them the junior commercial trainees or JCTs, more than 300 of whom were hired by the company between 1958 and 1971 and, after a two-year training program, were moved to permanent positions throughout the company.

While intakes of Junior Commercial Trainees would be destined to play an important role throughout the company from the 1960s and into the start of the 747 era, one of them, Keith Buls, could have been expected to win the undying thanks of one-time CEO Cedric Turner.

Much to the surprise of many in the company, the front page of the August 1962 *Qantas News* announced that Turner had won the £100,000 Opera House Lottery.

What the article didn't mention was that Keith Buls had actually purchased the ticket for him. Former human resources colleague Chris Kewley tracked Buls down recently: 'He told me he is still trying to spend the whole one pound he was given as thanks!'

Still other groups use their titles to keep their sense of humour alive, often with a tinge of Qantas irony. One such regular luncheon group, known as The Rorters, comprises former staff who were based in San Francisco in the 1970s, taking their name from an accusation by chief executive Keith Hamilton that they were 'rorting the system', via long lunches and dodgy expense accounts, and the issuing of free tickets to clients of 'questionable value'. Then there's the OAFs, or Old Airline Farts, who meet monthly at an inner-city hotel.

With this rich vein of empathy and nostalgia, there was much to draw from when the end of the 747 era in Qantas fortuitously coincided with the celebration of the centenary of the oldest airline in the English-speaking world. The 'Red Tail Road to 100' series of reunions was born out of the desire of a small group of the airline's former South Australian staff to celebrate the 50th anniversary of the opening of the Adelaide office in 1964. Such was the success of the reunion in 2014, which managed to attract 80 former staff members not only from Adelaide but across Australia, that one of the primary instigators, Rafael Toda, and three other former Qantas executives formed a foundation committee aimed at celebrating the airline's centenary in 2020.

Thus the Red Tail Road to 100 initiative was born. John Hudson Fysh, the son of the airline's founder, became the project's patron in memory of his father, and thirteen chapters were formed in all Australian states and overseas. Their task was to foster regular state reunions in the lead-up to two 'Grand Milestone Centenary' reunion events during the Qantas centenary.

Unfortunately, the onset of COVID-19 impacted plans for the actual centenary year of 2020. But in April 2021, with the support of current Qantas chief executive Alan Joyce, more than 150 Red Tail members, along with partners and guests, travelled by air, rail and road to the airline's Longreach birthplace to participate in four days of celebrations. This was followed by a final Grand Milestone event, again attracting more than 150 former and current airline staff at Qantas's Sydney headquarters, in April 2022, marking the retirement of the Red Tail Road to 100 initiative.

Yet its significance doesn't end there. Red Tail inspired the creation of yet another initiative: a non-profit organisation titled RU on Q, aimed at assisting former Qantas staff who face day-to-day challenges after life at Qantas. As Rafael Toda says, 'I'm sure Sir Hudson and Paul McGinness would be pleased.'

***

It's safe to say that the international prestige of the original Boeing company which produced the 747 no longer exists today. Although its more recent products, such as the 777 and 787, ply the skies, its reputation has suffered from the disastrous problems surrounding another of its aircraft, the Boeing 737. Seattle, the 747's birthplace, is no longer the accepted home of the company, and the corporate vision has shifted from a deeply engraved ethical and engineering focus to shareholder-driven returns.

Congressional inquiries and numerous books have in recent years chronicled the decline in standards and engineering oversight that has seen the company's reputation suffer a dramatic image turnaround from the days of Joe Sutter and his dedicated team. It's a situation that often leads to expressions of sadness when former Qantas staff gather to reminisce.

Perhaps the most tragic comparison relates to the shortcomings and fatal flaws built into the Boeing 737, revealed in the aftermath of the crashes involving Lion Air and Ethiopian Airlines. These played their part in the ascendancy of Boeing's traditional competitor, Airbus.

While history shows that Sutter's Boeing gambled the farm on the 747 idea, unlike their successors Sutter and his team never lost sight of their primary aim: make it work and bring its rewards, but ensure it flies safely. In that respect, Sutter was one of a breed easily recognised in Qantas: dedicated people who built the image and enhanced the reputation of the airline, in Australia and across the world.

ACKNOWLEDGEMENTS

To adequately thank all those who have helped me bring together the half-century of the Boeing 747's time in Qantas is a formidable task and, even if achievable without overlooking someone, would run to many pages.

Among those who have given me much of their time, along with their memories, have been David Forsyth, Gordon Power, John F. Ward, Jim Bradfield, Wayne Kearns, Norm King, Norm Leek, Michael Ryan, Max Hill, Harry Miller, the late Norm Field, and of course David Crotty, who is largely responsible for maintaining the record of the 747 years. And when it comes to the 747 itself in Qantas, special thanks are owed to Scott Collins, who in addition to being one of the small group of people over the years who oversaw deliveries of the aircraft from Seattle, set about the task of compiling *50 Years of Qantas 747 Aircraft*, a complete record of all 747 aircraft operated by the company. Not only does his catalogue profile each aircraft's delivery date and duration of its service but its Mean Takeoff Weight and engine type, from the first 747-200 in July 1971 to the last of the -400ER versions accepted by the company in July 2003. And as for the Qantas of today, my sincere thanks go to Group Chief Customer Officer Stephanie Tully, Amanda Bolger and their team who also reached out to help me trace people from so many years ago.

I do hope that those not mentioned here will accept my deep gratitude for their willingness to revisit a past that has left a lasting impression on so many of us privileged to have experienced it.

Sadly, many, like Bob Walker, who first doubted the concept of the 747 would ever work for Qantas but quickly began to grasp its significance, have passed but have left an indelible mark on the airline's 747 history. As Boeing's legendary Joe Sutter once said: 'They were the people we listened to!'

Even many others who subsequently moved on from the company would still retain that deep sense of pride at once being part of an airline and an aeroplane that reshaped Australia's commercial travel industry, or, as one of the airline's most memorable characters John Fordham succinctly put it: 'When it came to aviation in Australia, Qantas was the only game in town!'

Perhaps understandably, there will be some who might question the inclusion of a select band of media representatives in a book on the 747 era. Call it an author's indulgence but the fact is that while the relationship between the media and a high-profile company can be fraught, aviation writers, as they were then more widely known, came with a wider interest across all aspects of the industry generally. Occasionally, we had to confess, they kept us honest! Privatisation and the accompanying shareholder interest dramatically converted that relationship into a much more financial landscape.

As for the 747 era itself, certainly the developments in engine and airframe technology have exceeded anything achieved by the venerable jumbo but it's probably safe to say that none will ever match the image it has left with the airline or its passengers.

Once again I'm indebted to the team at Allen & Unwin and the encouragement and advice, firstly from Rebecca Kaiser and later her worthy successor Tom Bailey-Smith, along with copyeditor Emma Driver, who patiently turned some of my suspect sentence structures and split infinitives into a hopefully readable document!

And last, but certainly not least, my own family: my wife Jose, who once again combined her admirable patience with much helpful advice while managing to handle the frustrations of living with someone whose mind was so frequently distracted, and our son Steven and daughters Suzanne and Frances, all of whom constantly offered advice and encouragement. I hope too, as they travel future skies, our grandson Benjamin and granddaughter Emmanuelle can reflect on an Australian era we're unlikely to see again.

SOURCES

Books

Colin Burgess, *Laughter in the Air: Tales from the Qantas era*, Sydney: Colin Burgess Hutchinson, 1988.

Barry Cohen, *Life with Gough*, Sydney: Allen & Unwin, 1998.

Richard de Crespigny, *QF32*, Sydney: Pan Macmillan, 2012.

Sir Hudson Fysh, *Wings to the World: The story of Qantas 1945–1966*, Sydney: Angus & Robertson, 1970.

John Gunn, *High Corridors: Qantas 1954–1970*, Brisbane: University of Queensland Press, 1988.

Paul Holmes, *Daughters of Erebus*, Auckland: Hodder Moa, 2011.

Bruce Leonard, *A Tradition of Integrity*, Sydney: UNSW Press, 1994.

Colin Lock, *Finished with Engines: The story of Qantas' longhaul flight engineers 1941–2009*, Sydney: Colin Lock, 2013.

Ron Petrich and Norm Field, *Qantas Memories: Or how could you ever forget?*: Self-published, 2016.

Robert J. Serling, *Legend and Legacy: The story of Boeing and its people*, New York: St. Martin's Press, 1991.

Dick Smith, *My Adventurous Life*, Sydney: Allen & Unwin, 2021.
Mark Vanhoenacker, *Skyfaring: A journey with a pilot*, London:
Vintage, 2016.

Other sources

Aussie Airliners, R.N. Smith Collection, <www.aussieairliners.org>
Aircraft magazine
Kerri Grant, 'A high-flyer in war and peace', *Sydney Morning Herald*,
3 December 2004 <www.smh.com.au/national/a-high-flyer-in-war-and-peace-20041203-gdk8n4.html>
Qantas: Spirit of Australia, inflight magazine
Qantas News